THE
Rolling Stones
Unseen Archives

THE Rolling Stones
Unseen Archives

PHOTOGRAPHS
Daily Mail

SUSAN HILL

This is a Parragon Book
This edition published in 2003

Parragon
Queen Street House
4 Queen Street
Bath, BA1 1HE, UK

Photographs © Associated Newspapers Archive
Text © Parragon

Produced by Atlantic Publishing
Design and origination by Cambridge Publishing Management Ltd

A catalogue record for this book is available from the British Library.
ISBN 1-40541-587-8
Printed in China

Contents

	Page
Introduction	7
Acknowledgements	8
The Story So Far	9
1964–69	38
1970–74	142
1975–79	172
1980–84	214
1985–89	256
1990–2002	298
Chronology	359

Introduction

Almost forty years after they first strutted and glowered centre stage, the Rolling Stones still embody all that is bad, dirty, angry and sexy about rock 'n' roll. Some, whose reverence for jazz or blues musicians increases as the artist ages, still cling to the idea that it is undignified for rockers to keep on roaring. Yet the pulling power of the Rolling Stones continues to confound. Their audiences – by no means restricted to those who grew up with them – know how dangerously exciting a Stones concert can still be.

In the early 1960s the Stones seemed to stalk the Beatles, out-rousing the fans and out-shocking the parents. Just as there were Mods and Rockers, so there was often a divide between Beatles fans and Stones fans – before they realised it was possible to be both. But for a while the Rolling Stones made the Beatles seem tidy and safe. 'Let It Be', sang the Beatles sweetly. *Let It Bleed*, was the Stones reply. Raw and bruised energy was ever their style.

To have survived, let alone triumphed, for so long in a notoriously fickle industry speaks of art, guile, musicianship and planning, as well as skill at expressing and rousing primal instincts. And the right looks, of course. Mick's sulky look redefined male beauty. The tragically-doomed, blond Brian was always a fallen angel. Skeletal Keith with his black leather just looked so *dirty*, and Bill and Charlie so moody and cool. Later Mick Taylor and Ronnie Wood became Rolling Stones, and they helped the band grow old disgracefully and remain legendarily subversive.

This book charts the amazing career of the Rolling Stones, though a series of revealing photographs drawn from the *Daily Mail*'s comprehensive archive. The pictures are accompanied by perceptive captions which add context and depth to give a rounded and comprehensive portrait of the greatest rock 'n' roll band in the world.

Acknowledgements

The photographs in this book are from the archives of the *Daily Mail*.
They have been carefully maintained by the dedicated staff in the Picture Library
without whose help this book would not have been possible.

Particular thanks to Steve Torrington, Dave Sheppard, Brian Jackson, Alan Pinnock,
Paul Rossiter, Richard Jones and all the staff.

Thanks also to Karen Beaulah, Trevor Bunting, Julie Crane, John Dunne, Anthony Linden,
Tim Newton, Nicki Pendleton Wood, Cliff Salter, Sandra Stafford and Peter Wright.

THE
Rolling Stones
The Story So Far

CHAPTER ONE

Come On

In the early 1960s rock 'n' roll had been imported to Britain, mainly by merchant seamen who sailed between north America and Liverpool and, with the end of National Service, there was the glimmering of a youth culture. But it was very faint. Youthful virtue was still widely perceived in a 'short-back-and-sides' and obedient order. Public houses observed opening hours imposed during the First World War and almost the only outlets for teenagers' energies were youth clubs – often Church run – or school hall hops.

Elvis Presley was popular, perhaps in Britain because he had entered his post-GI ballad phase. But a few years earlier his music had been raunchy and had filtered down to London and south of the Thames from the Soho coffee bars where British beatniks hung out and from whence the careers of Brit rock 'n' rollers like Tommy Steele and Billy Fury had been launched.

It was across this canvas that the five young men who were to become the Rolling Stones were inspired to make their mark. After the 1963 Liverpool beat explosion, the Beatles and all the other groups in Brian Epstein's care, pop pundits attempted to generate a north/south pop civil war by declaring Dave Clark Five's 'London Sound' as the new big thing. The white-trousered and navy blazered lads from Tottenham did produce some stomping hits, but Dave Clark's greater satisfaction today may derive from having astutely acquired rights to the seminal TV pop programme *Ready, Steady, Go.*

If there *was* a London Sound it was the blues and R & B-influenced music that flourished in small clubs south of the Thames – particularly if there was an art school in the neighbourhood. At the time, art schools were popular destinations for many teenagers looking for further education. These schools often had a relaxed atmosphere and were great places to tune into music that was somehow more sophisticated and intelligent than pure pop. Some students would even carry around imported blues albums almost as a fashion item, like expensively imported American denims.

That's how Mick Jagger and Keith Richards, both still living with their parents, met early in 1962. An album sleeve was spotted during a train journey and cultural history was made as Keith headed towards art school and Mick to the London School of Economics, where he was studying for a degree. From that moment they were to become the two enduring constants of the Rolling Stones.

In fact, the two had overlapped at Wentworth County Primary School but barely noticed each other. Mick was born in Dartford, Kent into middle-class respectability on 26 July 1943. Keith was born nearby on 18 December

1943, his family background more working-class. The two found they had a mutual friend in Dick Taylor, with whom Mick played in a group called Little Boy Blue and the Blue Boys. Almost at once Keith also joined the band.

Brian Lewis Jones was born and raised in the gracious spa town of Cheltenham, Gloucestershire, on 28 February 1941. By the time he left school, aged seventeen, he had already fathered two children. He was also so widely proficient an instrumentalist in a local band (the Ramrods), that he was 'talent-spotted' by the legendary jazz musician Alexis Korner. Alexis invited Brian to stay at his flat during his escapes from Cheltenham to visit London clubs. Brian had already committed himself to a career in music and wanted to form a band.

In spring 1962, Korner's band, Blues Incorporated, played regularly at the Ealing Jazz Club. The band's drummer was a long-faced, quiet young man, Charlie Watts (born 2 June 1941 in Islington). Mick, Keith and Taylor made contact with Brian at the club after hearing him play slide guitar. Within weeks Mick, Keith, Dick Taylor, Brian and Charlie had begun jamming together, and Mick joined Blues Incorporated as a singer. Soon Mick, Keith and Brian took a small flat off Chelsea's King's Road, and the south London boys gradually ignited Brian's interest in R & B guitar and harmonica.

Meanwhile, Bill Wyman (born William Perks in Lewisham on 24 October 1936), had completed National Service (during which he'd learned to play guitar), married and worked as a storekeeper in Streatham. By 1962 he was playing bass guitar semi-professionally, backing mid-rank pop singers. He auditioned for the as yet un-named new band without great enthusiasm. It was only on hearing that the respected Charlie Watts was recruited that Bill decided to commit.

By June the band had named themselves The Rollin' Stones – as suggested by Brian and inspired by a Muddy Waters song. When they played at London's Marquee Club for the first time in July that year, they had become the Rolling Stones.

There are three legendary managers in British pop history: Brian Epstein, Malcolm Maclaren and Andrew Loog Oldham. Arguably the least holy of this remarkable trinity was Loog Oldham. Oldham, part Dutch-American, part English, was born in 1944 and became a product of the English public school system. Even as a teenager he was style and fashion-obsessed. He worked by day as a runner for Mary Quant and by night as a waiter at Soho's Flamingo Club. Then he worked in pop PR and, briefly, for Brian Epstein. After seeing the Rolling Stones in Richmond in April 1963, Loog saw the future and was determined to manage the band. He was young, hip and cool. He may have bleached his hair and he usually wore shades. He was nineteen years old. A month later, he signed the band. He kept them working hard in the clubs until they were good enough to stand a chance of getting a recording deal. In a little over a year they had done it.

The Rolling Stones' first single, 'Come On', was released on 7 June 1963. A cover of the old Chuck Berry song, it was a furious rant listing a series of teenage frustrations: wrong numbers, clapped-out cars and a lack of success with the opposite sex all made for dissatisfaction. 'Come On' made a brief appearance low in the June charts.

When the Stones performed on ABC-TV's *Thank Your Lucky Stars* wearing identical dark trousers, jackets and ties it was to be the first and last time the band dressed the same. But a template was set and stars were born. Brian, although still nominally the leader of the band, was prophetically upstaged by Mick's aggressively posturing vocals. Keith, as ever, managed to look both vulnerable and mean, while Charlie and Bill were cool and moody. In an era in which even the Beatles wore suits and all groups had a uniform of sorts, the Stones wore a disparate selection of clothes that might have been picked randomly from charity shops. Occasionally each sported a daring black leather waistcoat.

By the end of 1963 it was a case of 'lock up your daughters'! The Stones had begun to roll.

CHAPTER TWO
Little Red Roosters

No one could have predicted that one minor hit record (on Decca, with the record label still smarting at its folly at turning down the Beatles) would prove so significant. Pop acts were expected to fade fast. Even Ringo Starr, when questioned about his plans after 'She Loves You' (the Beatles' third UK No. 1 single), said he hoped to open a hairdressing salon soon. Mick Jagger was to negotiate a mere 'gap year' from the London School of Economics as the Stones' first major British tour began in September 1963.

A second tour opened in Harrow, near Charlie's former art school, early in January 1964. The band's first EP (extended play record), featuring four songs, was released later that month, and between live gigs there were radio and TV appearances. Work on a debut album progressed, with musicians like Graham Nash and Allan Clarke of Manchester's Hollies and American singer Gene Pitney sitting in on sessions. The album (known as *Rolling Stones*, but without any formal title on the cover) was released in April 1964. Meanwhile, the band searched for months for a follow-up to their first single.

Oldham had seen that there was a division between those fans who preferred the rough and raw approach of

the Stones and those who followed the cheerful mop-tops (whose melodies had even parents' toes tapping). The Stones had better be bad, dirty and dangerous enough to outrage parents as well as to thrill the daughters. News of Brian's early parenthood was great PR. So was an episode the following March, during which members of the band urinated against a garage forecourt wall having been refused entry to a lavatory. Oldham's masterstroke in publicising the band may well have been the line 'Would you let your daughter go out with one?'

In November 1963, the Stones' second single, 'I Wanna Be Your Man' was finally released. That the song was written by John Lennon and Paul McCartney, whose prodigious output enabled them to offer songs to rival

bands, scuppers any idea of some war between the Beatles and the Stones. In fact they were the best and most supportive of friends.

'I Wanna Be Your Man' stayed in the charts for thirteen weeks, and it possibly irritated Jagger and Richards (writing as Nanker and Phelge) that the boys in the other band were collecting writers' royalties. In any event, it was just a month later that Gene Pitney released a Jagger/Richard song (Keith had been advised to drop the final 's' from his name), 'That Girl Belongs To Yesterday', produced by Loog Oldham. Thereafter, the Stones increasingly recorded their own material.

'Not Fade Away' was released in February 1964 and reached No. 3 in the UK charts. Touring, including a relatively restrained foray in New York to promote 'Not Fade Away' (which charted for a few weeks in the States in May 1964), interviews, radio and TV, secured their immediate future. Despite accounting that enabled their record company to retain earnings for many months, each Rolling Stone was now committed to rock 'n' roll independence. Mick and Keith found their own places, and could run to better meals than eggs and potatoes. Brian had a flat in west London with his girlfriend and second son (although he spent time elsewhere). Bill got a mortgage for his wife and family. And Charlie soon added to this domestic harmony with new wife, Shirley.

On stage, though, they seemed more rebellious than ever. Longish hair for men was now accepted, so the Stones' hair had to be longer, lankier, seemingly dirtier. (Brian Jones actually washed his golden tresses at least twice a day, but Jagger declared in May 1964, the month after their first album release, that he only washed his once a week.) Accusations of incitement to civil insurrection did not appear to trouble them. There was no public contrition when, at Wembley Stadium in April 1964, thirty of 8,000 fans were arrested for riotous behaviour. Riots in Scotland over bootleg tickets followed, just as the album went to No. 1.

The pattern for the following three decades was set when yet another tour began in May 1964. There were more riots in Scotland and Mick's maracas became a temporary symbol for shaking convention. When the Stones flew to New York in early June pundits predicted that they would soon eclipse the Beatles. However, after two concerts at Carnegie Hall, Mick stated on 20 June that he gave the Stones another two years. Perhaps he was hedging his bets prior to the release of the band's new single 'It's All Over Now'. But he needn't have worried. By 8 July it was the UK's No. 1.

Throughout the rest of the year the band toured triumphantly and another EP, 'Five by Five', released in August kept fans happy. In September they were voted most popular group in a *Melody Maker* poll and 'Not Fade Away' was declared best single of the year. On 13 September in Liverpool, in an eerie preview of something that would take place in California many years later, the Stones had hired twenty-four rugby players to protect them at a concert. But some 5,000 fans still stormed towards the stage and overcame the guards. Four days later police dogs had to control 4,000 fans in Carlisle. On a sweeter note, Andrew Loog Oldham was married in Glasgow that month and Charlie wed Shirley Ann Shephard in Bradford a few weeks later.

The year rolled on with recordings, dates in Europe and further US concerts, including an appearance on Ed Sullivan's TV show. In their absence 'Little Red Rooster' was released in Britain in November 1964 and by the time the Stones were back in Britain for their *Ready, Steady, Go* TV slot the single was No. 1. Just before Christmas, Brian issued the first of many denials that he was leaving the band.

The Stones' second album was released in January 1965. Once again, and at Oldham's insistence, the sleeve showed just the band's faces with no title or mention of their name. The band's commitments early that year included recording in Los Angeles, then a series of concerts in Honolulu, Fiji, New Zealand and Australia. Before that, though, they had to meet old UK obligations in small venues, some of which had been cheaply contracted long before the band's current success. 'The Last Time', their fifth UK single, was released at the end of February 1965. It coincided with their return, yet another British tour, then concerts all over Europe and North America.

While in Hollywood in May that year, the band cut a Jagger/Richard song called '(I Can't Get No) Satisfaction'. It was based on a hard, fierce, daggered riff that Bill had experimented with. At the time, the band thought the song would be useful as an album filler. However, it would soon become their first US No. 1 single, the intro remaining one of the all-time rock 'n' roll classics.

The band's third album, *Out Of Our Heads*, was released in July 1965, around the time of their return from the US and the start of yet another tour. One month later Oldham announced the birth of Immediate – a record label that would, theoretically, enable Stones members to write and record their own material with few restrictions and increased royalty earnings. None the less, the Stones remained contracted to Decca for the release of the iconic '(I Can't Get No) Satisfaction' in August that year. It entered the UK charts on 26 August at No. 3 and held the No. 1 slot for three weeks.

There were short breaks for individual band members, more gigs, TV and further outrage. Hotels in Germany cancelled their reservations that autumn for fear of insurrection. Each band member must have been worn out, but they couldn't stop the momentum now. Brian had another son (by Linda Lawrence) to worry about, but nothing could stem the band's onward and upward drive. In late October, they released the clangingly discordant single 'Get Off Of My Cloud'. On the B side was the wistful and gently melancholic 'The Singer Not The Song', establishing a pattern of contrast in their singles. The Stones had defied the odds in remaining true to their original image, but were confident enough to display tender lyricism too.

Their north American fan base demanded yet another tour before the year's end and another pattern was set. The Rolling Stones have never forgotten the people who made them, and they increasingly recorded in and toured the US. Nothing could arrest their mercurial power now, not even tame British Christmas TV appearances that year. This had been a defining year for the Stones, closing with 'Satisfaction' being voted best single in the UK and USA, plus numerous other awards for being best group across a range of categories.

A generation had anticipated or learned about teenage pleasures to the soundtrack of the Rolling Stones' first recordings and for fans power escalated with every tour, TV appearance, chart single and album. By the end of 1965 the Rolling Stones were huge all over Europe and in the United States. They'd had three successful albums and a string of singles, which almost routinely topped the charts. There may have been the odd mutter of internal dissent, but the band was truly part of the rock establishment when another new year drew in.

CHAPTER THREE

Some Girls

There's no doubt that the behaviour of the Rolling Stones was responsible for an obsessive interest in the private lives of band members. Little was known about Bill, except that he was married to Diane. Decades later, when he published *Stone Alone*, based on meticulous diaries kept throughout his career as a Rolling Stone, he offered startling revelations about his adventures with young female fans while playing away from home. Charlie's 1964 marriage has proved to be steady as a rock, and jazz has remained his spare-time passion (evidenced by the 1965 publication of his book about Charlie Parker, *High Flying Bird*). Little is known of Keith's early romances. His demonically impish charm may have attracted many young women, but eventually he developed a relationship with a blond German actress named Anita Pallenberg.

Almost from the start, however, the affairs of Brian and Mick were played out in public. By spring 1963, Mick Jagger was stepping out with pretty brunette Chrissie Shrimpton, younger sister of the iconic 60s supermodel, Jean. The connection with the middle-class Shrimpton family exemplified Mick's enduring penchant for lofty thoroughbred beauties even as he was class rebellion personified. The relationship with Chrissie lasted for more than two years and in June 1965 the pair were rumoured to be considering marriage. But it was volatile, then doomed once Mick fell for the daughter of a baroness …

Marianne Faithfull may have lived in provincial Reading, but her ancestors had glittered at imperial courts and waltzed with Vienna's finest. Her mother, Eva, had been a ravishing, stateless beauty when Glyn Faithfull, a wartime officer in British Intelligence, rescued her. Marianne was born in 1947 and lived in Lancashire until her parents separated. The little house in Reading was a shrine to a noble past, and convent-educated Marianne grew up amid sophistication, culture and taste.

At seventeen, Marianne was an astonishing beauty with a lovely, slightly husky, singing voice. Her potential had been spotted at a party by Oldham, who suggested that Mick and Keith write a song for her. By 1964 she was involved with Cambridge undergraduate and later art dealer John Dunbar. They would marry and have a son, Nicholas. Soon after the sweetly melancholy 'As Tears Go By' charted for her that summer, she and Mick were to become an item. They reigned supreme as rock's defining couple for nearly six years.

But while Mick seemed to thrive on life at the edge and even on scandal, Marianne was fragile. Eventually,

after a miscarriage in 1968, a botched suicide attempt the following year, the hurt of Mick's affair with the singer/actress Marsha Hunt in 1969 and a series of drug-related crises, Marianne found the will and strength to leave Mick.

The story of Keith and Anita overlaps with that of Mick and Marianne – and begins with Brian. Remembering those times, it's relevant to note that, even with the introduction of the birth control pill, it was somehow men who were most liberated in the climate of new sexual freedom. Jagger/Richard lyrics of the mid-sixties from the wonderful 'Under My Thumb' and 'Stupid Girl' on the *Aftermath* album to 'Out of Time', also written in 1966 and gloriously bellowed by Chris Farlowe on an irresistible hit single later that year, expertly make the point – ironically expressing the old love 'em and leave 'em chauvinism.

Brian had luxuriant fair hair and a 'lost boy' aura that alternated with an equally appealing aloof glamour. It was understandable if, at times, he seemed almost sulky on stage as he stood motionless with his guitar clamped across his chest. He had, after all, thought he was the leader of the Rolling Stones until he'd been eclipsed by Mick. None the less, thousands of girls adored him. And at least three of them bore him sons.

Brian's first child was born to a fourteen year-old girl when he was (aged sixteen) still at school. Still in his home town, three years later, Brian fathered another son, who

was named Julian Mark after his jazz hero 'Cannonball' Adderley. Soon after the Stones' first success, a third son was born; the mother was a young model. When Brian cited his hobbies as bus and train spotting (he did indeed acquire two double-deckers, which he gave to a museum), some girls might have begged to differ.

Emotionally, he met his nemesis with the formidable Anita Pallenberg in 1965. Their relationship was riven with widely reported upsets, but he never recovered from the breakdown of that relationship, particularly since it was Keith to whom she fled three years later. It seems that other girlfriends such as Suki Poitier – the socialite survivor of the car crash that killed Guinness heir Tara Browne, elegised in John Lennon's 'A Day In The Life' – and Anna Wohlin, the young Swede who was with him at the end, never really reached him in the same way.

So everyone knew that each of the Rolling Stones had sex lives. Those of the two married members of the band elicited no comment. But even as recently as the mid-60s the very idea of single men and women having sex still had the power to shock. This bewildering moral paradox suited the Rolling Stones very well. With every year that passed they seemed to outwit the notion that rebels and rock 'n' rollers live fast and die young. That illusion ended with the fate of Brian Jones. But in the meantime the band appeared charmed in their ability to embody the furious sexual energies of the young.

CHAPTER FOUR

The Chelsea Drug Store

The Chelsea Drug Store on the King's Road had a pharmacy upstairs, but unless you had a late night prescription to collect it was more of a café/diner in which to preen and be seen. However, the name and the *idea* of the place was less innocent, evocative of New York's Chelsea Hotel, where rock stars and writers had glamorous parties. Throughout the mid-60s, with at least three Stones living within posing distance, there was always the hope that one of them might choose that day to 'go down to the Chelsea Drug Store', as Mick was to sing on the single 'You Can't Always Get What You Want'. The place somehow became emblematic of the band's fortunes over the next few years.

The year 1965 had begun with more touring, TV shows and the band's second album (*Rolling Stones No. 2*) entering the charts at No. 1 in late January. Consolidating the band's success was 'The Last Time', their fifth UK single, which topped the charts by the end of March. That month, on a tour date in Manchester, the Stones were ejected from their hotel for not observing the dress code. A few days later, the trade magazine *Tailor and Cutter* implored the band to wear ties. It claimed many retailers

were going out of business because young men were following their example. Mick retorted that ties didn't just dangle in the soup, they could help a fan take a potentially dangerous grip.

The band provoked further anger in April that year. They refused to stand and wave on the revolving stage, part of the traditional finale of *Sunday Night at the London Palladium*, Britain's top TV variety show. North America's equivalent TV show, the *Ed Sullivan Show*, relaxed a veto it had on the band, and allowed them to perform in May, mid-way through the Stones' US tour. Towards the end of that tour, the Stones pipped the Beatles to come top for the first time in an American pop poll.

There was to be trouble at home, though. In early July, just before their third album, *Out Of Our Heads*, was released, summonses were issued against Mick, Brian and Bill for 'insulting' behaviour concerning the incident in March when, unable to use the lavatory, the boys had resorted to urinating against a wall of a petrol station forecourt in Essex. They were later fined £5 apiece and costs.

That summer a few faint rumblings threatened to challenge the stability of the band. Bill began producing records for other acts and Mick announced in New York that the entire British music scene had become boring. But then, with 'Satisfaction' topping the UK singles charts

in August, a new agent (Tito Burns) and a new five-year recording deal with Decca, any fears that they were splitting up were dampened.

The band kicked into a new British tour in late September, just before the release of 'Get Off Of My Cloud'. By November, the record was simultaneously No. 1 in Britain and the USA. Towards the end of their US tour, in December, Anita flew to join Brian in California, although rumours of an impending marriage were denied. They spent Christmas together in the Virgin Islands.

The year 1966 must have opened with a glow as polls on both sides of the Atlantic had variously named 'Satisfaction' best single of the previous year and the Stones best band. Added to that, by February their ninth UK single, 'Nineteenth Nervous Breakdown' was headed for No. 1. However, they continued with a punishing schedule of touring and fans continued to riot – the band often held responsible for incitement. They continued to be barred from hotels as managers feared for security and peace for other guests.

One of their finest albums, *Aftermath*, was released in April 1966. In May plans for a film, *Only Lovers Left Alive*, were announced: The Stones would star as individual actors but record the soundtrack as a band. The film never progressed, but Mick's enduring interest in cinematic projects may have been ignited then. 'Paint It Black' was

released the same month – its Indian influences inspiring *Melody Maker*'s Chris Welch to describe it as pop's greatest ever 'punch up the Punjab'. This single made it to No. 1 in both the UK and USA.

After all the touring and recording it was a shame that Brian's summer holiday in Morocco was ruined by a broken hand, leading to fears that he wouldn't play for two months. But by September the band was ready to go out and promote their new single, 'Have You Seen Your Mother Baby, Standing In The Shadow' – the picture sleeve of which showed the band in 1940s drag. Bill, dressed in female army uniform, is in a wheelchair. The accompanying promotional film was banned by the BBC. Brian managed to trump this with Anita in November, when posed wearing Nazi SS uniform with a doll crushed beneath his jack-booted foot.

The band were busy recording in London as the year closed, their compilation album *Big Hits (High Tide And Green Grass)* set to storm the Christmas charts. It was not to be a very happy Christmas for Mick and Chrissie Shrimpton, who broke up shortly beforehand. She was traumatised enough to attempt suicide. Mick was in love with Marianne Faithfull by then.

'Let's Spend The Night Together', released in January 1967, proved that nothing could stifle the Stones' bold exuberance, the uncompromising lyrics reinforcing their bad-boy image. The B side, 'Ruby Tuesday', was yet another gem, reminding everyone that the Beatles weren't the only band who never offered a weak B side. *Between The Buttons*, the new LP, was high in the charts by the end of the month.

With the dawning of the age of Aquarius in 1967, or, at any rate, the 'summer of love', there sometimes seemed to be no Stone unturned-on. A newspaper report in February stated that Mick had taken LSD and hash, which led to him taking out a libel action. The result was a summer blighted by a series of drug busts. The most celebrated – or notorious – episode took place at Keith's moated Sussex house in February. It resulted in a court case in which Keith was charged with allowing his premises to be used for the consumption of illegal

Love You' in August was widely supposed to contain a message of ironic forgiveness to the Establishment. Throughout all this Brian had his own drugs-related court case pending. A prison sentence imposed in December was set aside on medical grounds and he was placed on probation instead.

Within a simple song lyric about going down to the Chelsea Drug Store, the Rolling Stones could make fans feel guilty of no greater crime than wearing floral trousers. And, for the price of a trendy salad, the fans could at least be an extra part of the sideshow. Purple Hearts, or amphetamines, were assumed to be the Mods' drug of choice but few actually took them. None the less, drugs would appear to have been a fashion item – and that

substances and Mick for possession (even though only traces of an amphetamine legally purchased abroad the previous year were found). Although innocent of any offence, Marianne was effectively tried for the much-publicised 'crime' of being wrapped in a fur rug when the police raided.

Before the trial various Rolling Stones and girlfriends visited Morocco. When Anita returned to London with the others it was the end of her affair with Brian, the start of a new one with Keith and of tensions that eventually led to Brian leaving the band. Meanwhile Mick's and Keith's drugs case was heard and both were given prison sentences, causing a public outcry. The sentences were quashed on appeal in July and the release of the single 'We

wasn't the Rolling Stones' fault, even if they did not object to being associated with the culture and wrote songs that acknowledged it.

By the end of 1968 the Stones had not merely nursed their notoriety but increased it. At the same time Mick, and Keith Richard had become respected lyricists, and the musicianship of the entire band was much more complex, assured and professional than when they first formed. Mick was almost married to the ethereal Marianne and talking of a future in films. The others were also diversifying, and 'Time Is On My Side', a track from the album *Rolling Stones No. 2*, seemed apt. However, by 1968 it was more the case of borrowing time than having time on their side.

CHAPTER FIVE

Men of Wealth and Taste

If the Rolling Stones can be said to have had a bad year, that 'year' spanned 1967 to 1969. The more flamboyant trio within the band would be reduced to the indestructible partnership (song-writing and otherwise) of the Glimmer Twins (a nickname given to Mick and Keith). It would seem that three was a crowd and Brian was the classic accident waiting to happen.

In December 1967 the Stones – on their mettle – had released *Their Satanic Majesties Request* as an answer to the Beatles' album *Sergeant Pepper's Lonely Hearts Club Band*. Where the Beatles had dressed in satin tin-soldier outfits on their album sleeve, the Rolling Stones took the pantomime theme several steps further and posed in wizards' outfits. However, while *Sergeant Pepper* instantly became a defining classic, few would argue that the Stones' album (mockingly titled to remind us of the commands printed on the stiff blue passport that every travelling Briton carried at the time), was their finest. Two songs ('She's A Rainbow' and 'Two Thousand Light Years From Home') were marvellous, but perhaps the others were a little disappointing.

Brian's heart may not have been in it at the time. He had long resented Mick apparently becoming leader of the band. He'd lost his girlfriend to Keith and he was increasingly drawn towards musical interests that weren't shared by the others. Other band members also developed personal interests. In particular, in May 1968 Mick had announced his starring role in Nicolas Roeg's film *Performance*. This diversification didn't threaten the band, but a cloudy impression remains that Brian was allowed to go his own way.

For a while, 1968 seemed to be business as usual. 'Jumpin' Jack Flash' made No. 1 in June, its success certainly speeded by a short promotional film (an early version of a rock video). 'Street Fighting Man', their next US single, which was a track from the forthcoming *Beggars' Banquet* album, was banned in Chicago in September after recent riots at the Democratic Convention.

Earlier that year, student riots had seen barricades erected in Paris and students rioting across the world in protest at America's involvement in the Vietnam war. Mick 'went down to the demonstration' (yet another lyric from 'You Can't Always Get What you Want') outside the US embassy in Grosvenor Square, London. In less than a year

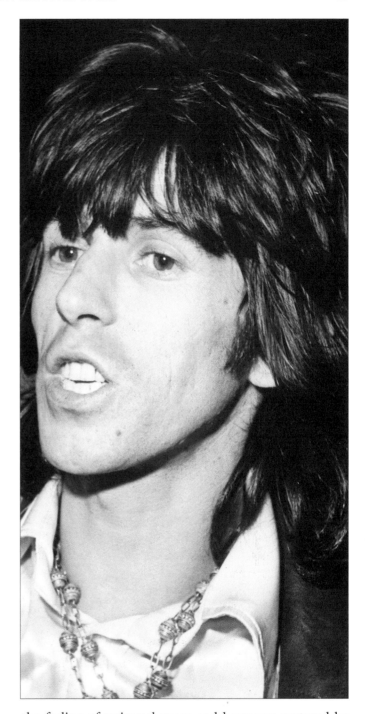

the feeling of universal peace and harmony captured by the Beatles' single 'All You Need Is Love' (on which some members of the Stones had sung in a studio performance), had evaporated.

Controversy had also stalked *Beggars' Banquet* in Britain, but in a different way. Its release was delayed until December 1968 as the original sleeve, which depicted a graffiti-covered lavatory, was banned and replaced by a dignified parody of a formal invitation card.

In October a delighted Mick and Marianne announced her pregnancy. However, she lost the baby on 20 November. Brian, meanwhile, purchased Cotchford

Farm (once the home of A.A. Milne, author of the *Winnie the Pooh* books) in Sussex around the same time. A week later *Beggars' Banquet* was released in the USA amid rumours that the band were splitting even though a new world tour was being planned. The year ended with the Stones voted best R & B band in the *New Musical Express* poll.

Throughout 1968, the inspired brilliance behind Brian's muffled xylophones that had introduced 'Under My Thumb', his fierce lead guitar, and the percussion and brass undertows that shaped many other tracks, seemed increasingly absent. Just as the Beatles were finding last ways of papering over their cracks, which, after five sublime years, were beginning to widen, similar fault lines in the foundations of the Rolling Stones were forming. In fact, early draftings of a plan that would eventually seek to buy Brian out of the Rolling Stones for a sum of money that would ultimately cover half his debts (had he lived to receive it) were privately considered as the very fabric of the Rolling Stones was corroding.

Heartbreak, despair, disappointment, jealousy, betrayal and a fresh series of drug busts all conspired to crush Brian as his dreadful destiny called. Depressed and in debt, he retreated to his farmhouse in Sussex.

Keith and Anita had confounded sceptics by settling into something resembling steady domesticity. Charlie and Bill had always had their own peaceful places of marital escape. By the end of 1968, Brian seemed to be very isolated.

CHAPTER SIX
Not Fade Away

The new year began dismally for Brian. Now alone in Sri Lanka, he was declined admission to several hotels whose managers mistook him for a penniless beatnik. Back in England, he was to spend ever more time at Cotchford Farm. It wasn't a large house but it was spacious enough and there was a lovely untamed garden and a swimming pool. Brian was a keen swimmer so the pool was a plus and the farm itself provided him with peace, space and calm.

Early in 1969 work began on a new album, with recording in both London and Italy. But progress was slow as Mick was also committed to writing the soundtrack of the Kenneth Anger film *Invocation Of My Demon Brother*. As well as that, he and Marianne were discussing roles in a forthcoming Australian movie, *Ned Kelly*. Furthermore, in May the pair were arrested for possession of cannabis at home in Chelsea. A few days later, Keith and a heavily pregnant Anita were involved in a car crash in Sussex. Anita broke her collar bone but a son, Marlon, was safely born in London on 10 August. Meanwhile, Bill and Diane Wyman's marriage had been quietly disintegrating, and their divorce was announced early in July.

Amid this climate of stress and diversification it was agreed at Cotchford Farm in early June that Brian and the

Stones should part company. 'Musical differences' was the reason given to explain the split. Two days later a tall, young, blonde, vegetarian, teetotaller called Mick Taylor was appointed as the band's new lead guitarist.

On the night of 2 July, the day after Mick and Marianne's drug hearing was adjourned, and exactly three weeks after leaving the band, Brian Jones' body was found at the bottom of his swimming pool. He had been drinking prior to a midnight swim and frequently resorting to his asthma inhaler. The coroner returned a verdict of death by drowning under the influence of drugs and alcohol. But wild rumours of more sinister events circulated almost at once and are still occasionally aired. He was just twenty-seven.

The Rolling Stones had planned a free concert in Hyde Park on Saturday 4 July to introduce Mick Taylor to fans and as a celebration of moving on. Despite Brian's death, the band insisted that the show should go ahead. It was a hot day and the park heaved with about 300,000 kaftan-clad flower children. Mick wore loose trousers and a white top with a flouncy skirt fastened with ribbons.

Towards the end of the concert he recited lines from Shelley's *Adonais*:

'Peace, peace! He is not dead, he doth not sleep –
He hath awakened from the dream of life ...'

He then opened boxes and released thousands of white butterflies into the blazing blue skies. It was said that many butterflies had suffocated in the boxes and that clouds of the escapees caused havoc in the gardens of south London later that day.

Four days later, in Australia, Marianne overdosed and sank into a five-day coma. That the Stones' single 'Honky Tonk Women' (which was later to win a BBC poll as best single of the year) hit the charts soon after may have been small compensation for a month of extraordinary strain and tragedy. Brian was buried on 10 July at the Cheltenham church where he had sung as a choirboy. The priest read from a telegram that Brian had recently sent to his parents. It said: 'Please don't judge me too harshly.'

The new Rolling Stones might have hoped that the rest of the year would quietly fade away. Mick had Marianne to look after and a film to make. Keith jammed with Eric Clapton and Ginger Baker on a single produced by George Harrison, Billy Preston's 'That's The Way God Planned It'. And, in the absence of completed new material, the band released a greatest hits album, *Through The Past Darkly (Big Hits Vol. 2)*. But perhaps the very worst was looming when they flew to Los Angeles in October to mix the new album and prepare for an American tour, which promised to be a sell-out.

Things had so far gone to plan coast to coast. On their final date of the tour, 6 December, some 500,000 fans amassed for a free concert at the Altamont Speedway Stadium in California. The concert was policed by Hell's Angels, who were paid in beer. They took their duties seriously. By the time the Stones made their customary late appearance, the crowd was a riotous assembly, the Angels beating teenagers with billiard cues. The show went on even when one Angel pulled a knife on a fan who managed to jump on stage. Two fans were killed when a car ploughed through the crowds; a third drowned in a ditch. There were hundreds of injuries.

This horrible year closed with the release of *Let It Bleed* in early December (a huge success on both sides of the Atlantic), Mick being fined for possession of cannabis, Marianne's acquittal, her holiday in Rome with an Italian film producer, Home Office pressure on Anita to marry (Keith, presumably) because of her alien immigrant status and two London Christmas shows at the Lyceum Ballroom in the Strand, where fans were showered with artificial snow.

CHAPTER SEVEN

Exiles on Main Street

And so the decade turned. But would the Rolling Stones turn over a new leaf? Some fans may have hoped the band would remain unrepentantly subversive. Many fans were also approaching the advanced age of thirty and almost needed the iconic rebels they'd grown up with to stay wickedly cool.

None the less, 1970 was relatively quiet – with a range of emotional rescues and bruises to be nursed. Mick and Marianne's long-term love affair was wilting, and Mick had begun to date other women – including the singer and actress Marsha Hunt (who bore him a daughter, Karis) – to take his mind off Marianne and the generally poor reviews given to *Ned Kelly*. By contrast, Keith Richard was

that month, around the time that Mick began dating Bianca Perez Morena de Macia. The new album reached No. 1 two months later.

Meanwhile, Mick endured another disappointment when Warner Brothers shelved the distribution of *Performance* in the USA believing American audiences would not be able to understand his British accent. This curious claim must have been irksome to a man whose singing voice had been hitting the spot Stateside for some years. Perhaps the studio was concerned about how middle-class America might react to the film in the wake of the Altamont concert. Certainly when the band played live that year it was mainly in Europe, where demand for tickets was reassuringly high.

There were no serious scandals or busts in 1970. Mick punched a reporter in Rome for 'asking stupid questions', but that was about the extent of it. The contract with

increasingly settled with Anita and Marlon. Bill Wyman was presumably recovering from his divorce and Charlie kept quiet, as ever. Sadly, Mick Taylor began a descent into a fondness for drugs that eventually worried him enough to find the strength to quit the Stones.

On 2 September that year, a new European tour began in Helsinki and an album recording finished. *Get Yer Ya Yas Out!* had been cut slowly and not released until 10 October. Marianne was divorced from John Dunbar later

Decca expired and the Stones, relishing the freedom that a label of their own could offer, began work on a new album.

Public interest grew in Bianca Perez Morena de Macia. She was variously described as a former Paris hotel chambermaid, and the multi-lingual daughter of a Nicaraguan diplomat. She was neither, although her family had powerful political connections and she had been a political science student in Paris, where she had briefly dated Michael Caine.

Bianca was a stunning Latin beauty and could have been Jagger's ravishing twin sister. But rather as Yoko Ono and Linda Eastman would be unfairly blamed for the Beatles' split, the British public did not take well to Bianca's presence on the Stones' periphery. They somehow got the idea that she had ousted Marianne Faithfull (who was, in fact, relieved and happy to have moved on). But Mick was enchanted, and Bianca was with him virtually everywhere he performed. The other Stones' wives and women friends did not seem to warm to her, either. Anita, the most long-standing partner of a Rolling Stone after the reticent Shirley Watts, may well have felt put out by the attention Bianca received. Rose Taylor and Bill Wyman's Swedish girlfriend Astrid Lundstrom were equally put off by Bianca's lofty detachment.

As Mick's commitment to Bianca deepened, work on the new *Sticky Fingers* album was hampered, to the dismay of some others in the band. But it was the 'real thing', and Mick and Bianca were to marry in St Tropez the following year. When the news reached Marianne, she was so startled that, despite her certainty that she and Mick were best apart, she fainted in a restaurant near Paddington where she had dazedly ordered food before catching a train to visit her mother.

The American release just before Christmas 1970 of *Gimme Shelter*, a film about the Altamont tragedy, had restored something of the Stones' bad-boy image – even though Keith Richard associated himself with a charity for drug addicts and offenders at the London premier of *Performance* in the new year. *Performance* was never granted a general release. It remains a cult classic and invariably fills art-house cinemas.

In the new year, the USA's *Billboard* voted the Rolling Stones third best artists of the previous decade. But even this didn't stop them giving a farewell tour. This announcement supported rumours that the band were to leave Britain to become reluctant tax exiles on some main street in France. The result was a stampeding demand for tickets for their concerts. As we know, the band have toured often since, but seldom again claiming it would be for the last time.

Any suggestion that the Rolling Stones were moving to escape vast tax debts was scotched, as was the idea that they no longer felt quite admired enough in Britain. The move was, their press agent insisted, simply because they loved France. They would still record in England and did not wish to relinquish British citizenship.

The farewell tour finished in London in March 1970, just as the same trade magazine that had earlier implored Mick to wear ties voted him one of the 100 best-dressed men in the world. After a couple of TV shows and a sparkling party in sedate Maidenhead, the band decamped to the South of France. Some eleven years later Bill Wyman was to record his single '(Si Si) Je Suis Un Rock Star', a funny and possibly ironic tribute to this particular part of their lives.

Wives, partners, children and staff spent a healing time in France. Photographs of their separate houses show elegant and graceful interiors, terrace tables strewn with the debris of meals for up to twenty, overflowing ashtrays, opened bottles, children running about and adults in casual clothes, rather like an extended family party. But there *was* work in progress and Mick *did* marry Bianca in St Tropez in May 1971. However, some Stones missed England and planned to return. Despite their relocation to France, the band remained as popular as ever in Britain with the release of *Sticky Fingers* in May (the sleeve designed by Andy Warhol and featuring a gentleman's well-packed jeans' crotch) and the hit single 'Brown Sugar' (which jangled a number of sensitive feminist nerves). Both single and album went on to top the UK and US charts.

Mick and Bianca's marriage had gained worldwide interest. She was well into her pregnancy with their daughter Jade (who was born in Paris that October) and didn't look radiantly happy in the photographs. That could have been because she resented the *paparazzi* intrusions. She and Mick both wore white suits, and their guests included Mr and Mrs Paul McCartney and Lord Lichfield, the Queen's cousin. UK media attention intensified whenever the pair visited Britain. Bianca's habitual claim that she spoke no English and her refusal to be a standard rock chick only deepened the public's fascination for the woman who had seemingly made an honest man out of Mick.

Meanwhile, plans were laid for a major new tour of the USA and there were recordings in Los Angeles. Anita was pregnant again and the Jagger newly weds were house-hunting on the West Coast as this most sober of Rolling Stones years drew to a close. Their relative lack of activity left their fans hungrier than ever. By and large the band had kept out of trouble since Brian's death but had still cleverly managed to retain the public's attention. These hadn't necessarily been vintage times. But it had given the Stones time to conserve their energy and gather some motivation for their next moves.

Just as the 1960s didn't really begin until well into the decade, the 1970s also took their time to ignite. Far from being the dull decade that some dismiss, the 70s were raunchy and exciting, and the restored Rolling Stones were ready to prove they were up for it all.

CHAPTER EIGHT
All Over Now?

In January 1972, Britain's *New Musical Express* voted the Rolling Stones second best British band and second best vocal band in the world. After all these years of being voted 'the best' it must have been hard for them to settle for less.

Over the next few years the Stones proved that they were still the greatest rock 'n' roll band in the world. They weren't deterred when another anthology album, *Milestones*, only charted at No. 17. After all, any true fan would already have all the tracks contained on the LP. The band answered back with the single 'Tumbling Dice', released on their own Rolling Stones label. It went into the British charts at once and reached No. 5 in May. Just weeks earlier Anita Pallenberg had given birth to a daughter, Dandelion, in Switzerland.

In the mid-1970s a British Airways advertising campaign featured a stewardess with a fly-hither look in her eye and the legend 'Want to get off with me?' Ten years earlier the Rolling Stones had suggested 'Let's Spend The Night Together'. It had taken the mainstream nearly a decade to catch up with the bold appeal of sexual realities. By then the Stones had moved further along their own path. And there were still kicks to be had, and delivered. The May 1972 release of the *Exile On Main*

Street double album, for example, stayed in the album charts for fourteen weeks, holding the No. 1 position for part of that time.

In the early 1970s Britain was getting used to metrification, worrying about the European Union, enjoying a TV sitcom called *The Good Life* and wondering whether platform soles made you look silly. People were listening to bands like the Faces, Jackson Five and the Osmonds. Bruce Springsteen cut his first album in New York in 1972. These were the times, and the Rolling Stones had to move with them even though they might never again define them.

Everything was looking good for the new US tour, which kicked off in June 1972. However, in July Keith was arrested for assault and Mick was arrested for obstructing a police officer after a scuffle at an airport stop-over while on the way to Boston. They were both called to appear before the Rhode Island court in December.

During the tour, Mick's performance outfit of slinky-tight and strategically zipped or laced lycra jumpsuits, which were studded with rhinestones and worn with tooled belts or floating silks tied around the hips, became a uniform. A wide expanse of hairless chest was usually revealed. Mick explained that he would have preferred to wear denims, but that even the most broken-in jeans did not allow the flexibility needed for his performance

athletics. Perhaps he changed from his spandex for his twenty-ninth birthday party after the final concert, at Madison Square Gardens, New York on 26 July. Guests included Truman Capote and Princess Lee Radziwill (Jacqueline Onassis' sister), Bob Dylan, Andy Warhol and Carly Simon. Carly's single 'You're So Vain', released later that year, was widely thought to have been inspired by Mick – who actually provided guest back-up vocals.

A few days later, Mick announced that he would retire from rock music at the age of thirty-three. He would not, he declared, stay in show business at all when he quit rock 'n' roll. In the meantime, though, his schedule included a month of recording in Jamaica (starting in late November 1972) and a tour of the Far East in the new year.

Just before Christmas 1972, an earthquake devastated Managua, Nicaragua – home of Bianca Jagger's relatives. Mick and Bianca chartered a jet from Jamaica to Managua to make a search for her family. She was not to find her parents until 31 December. The couple also took some 2,000 anti-typhoid syringes. This act was to signal Bianca's later work as a dedicated campaigner for international aid. It is also in contrast with the public's image of her as being a hedonist and aloof. However, a rather different international community – that of 2,000 fashion editors – *did* vote Mick and Bianca as being among the best-dressed people of 1972 in an American poll. When, a few days later, *Billboard* magazine voted the Stones the best band of the year, it looked like being runners-up had been a freak blip.

Despite the first-class travel and luxury hotels, touring was tiring – even punishing at times. It must take real effort to perform with energy and excitement for a new audience night after night, yet the Rolling Stones have never been slackers here. Australasia, Europe, the USA, and painstaking hours in even the best studios can't always have been a party. The Stones worked hard to keep their fans happy. Throughout the early and mid-70s their schedule was relentless. They even planned to be the first British band to tour the Soviet Union.

But they still seemed to make the news for the wrong reasons. Mick faced a new legal challenge when Marsha Hunt filed a claim in London about his responsibilities towards her daughter. Mick requested blood tests and eventually accepted paternity of Karis, settling an undisclosed sum with Marsha the following year. He had never shirked interim maintenance payments.

Keith was in different trouble in the summer of 1973, charged not only with possession of cannabis

but also with having a revolver and ammunition. He was remanded on bail, but was absent from court as he and Anita dealt with the aftermath of a fire at their Sussex home.

As the decade rolled on, the band's profile stayed high. Still the albums kept coming and still the fans queued for tickets to the regular tours. Not only that, the odd controversy over cover artwork or 'obscene' lyrics kept the band's rebellious image bright. It may only have been rock 'n' roll, but the British fans still liked it. So did the Japanese, who, in 1974, heaped plaudits on the Rolling Stones in general and Mick in particular.

Rumours also kept the fans entertained. There was the one about Mick and Bianca's marriage being shaky. Then there was the one about Mick Taylor's likely departure from the band. There was also the legendary tale of Keith being given a complete blood transfusion in Switzerland in August 1974. This, so the rumour went, was to make sure he was 'clean' next time he wished to enter the USA.

As it happens, Taylor did leave the Stones at the end of the year, joining Cream-founder Jack Bruce in his new band. Everyone involved was concerned that the split was

amicable. But stories persisted that Taylor had been unhappy about the lack of credit (and therefore perhaps royalties?) for his contribution to some songs. After many denials, his place in the band was taken in April 1975 by Ronnie Wood. Despite the arrangement being temporary, with Ronnie 'on loan' from the Faces, he remains with the band to this day.

Weeks later, the Stones embarked on their biggest-ever tour, playing to 1.5 million people at fifty-eight concerts across the Americas. Mid-tour, in June, Anita was deported from Keith's home in Jamaica on drugs charges. Weeks later, Keith was arrested in Arkansas for possessing an offensive weapon (he said it was a tin opener with an extra device for removing stones from horses' hooves).

Another exhausting year of tour dates and recording sessions ended with further accolades. In the USA, *Creem* magazine voted the Stones the best group, best R & B group and best live band. The droll and likeable Ronnie Wood won the magazine's award for most valuable musician, and the album compilation *Made In The Shade* was voted best re-issue. *It's Only Rock 'n' Roll* was voted best album and *Ladies And Gentlemen, The Rolling Stones*, best rock movie.

In spring 1976, Anita gave birth to a second son, Tara, named for Tara Browne, the Guinness heir whose death had inspired John Lennon's 'A Day In The Life'. Sadly, the baby died ten weeks later. After these difficult times for Keith and Anita, Dandelion was cared for by Keith's mother, Doris.

On 19 May, Keith crashed his Bentley in Buckinghamshire. Police found 'substances', later identified as LSD and cocaine, in the wreckage and he was remanded to appear in court in September. Despite all this, he and the band played on and toured, capitalising on the success of their most recent album, *Black And Blue*, released in April 1976.

In October 1976, amid strengthening rumours about the fragility of his marriage, Mick Jagger told *Woman's Own* (his interview being something of a *coup* for a magazine better known for its recipes and knitting patterns) that he had married for something to do, that he'd never been madly, deeply in love. Whether it was true or not, perhaps this is something that might better have been kept private.

CHAPTER NINE

Keith Don't Go

In 1977, Queen Elizabeth II was celebrating twenty-five years as head of state and commonwealth. Her Silver Jubilee year became one in which punk changed the face of rock music. The Stones would have to guard against looking out of touch with youth culture as bands like the Sex Pistols began to have a massive impact.

Indeed, the year began with the almost quaintly traditional sequence of drug-related court appearances for Keith, a wrangle with newspapers about the release of censored photographs, a new record deal (with Britain's ultra-establishment EMI) and Bill weakly complaining to a newspaper about how tiresome it was to find groupies lurking in hotel bathrooms when one checked in on tour.

Then appropriately enough, in February, the Stones flew to Canada for yet another tour. There was little surprise when Anita and Keith were detained at Toronto customs. Cannabis and traces of heroin were found, and Anita was arrested then released. Three days later the pair were arrested for possession of heroin at their hotel but were released and Keith bailed (albeit facing the threat of a life sentence).

Their first Canadian gig took place on 4 March at a club with an audience of only a few hundred. Afterwards,

a party was thrown for the band by Margaret Trudeau, the glamorous young wife of Canada's premier Pierre Trudeau. She had taken a suite at the band's hotel. Mrs Trudeau attended further concerts in Canada and arranged at least one more private party for the band, apparently unconcerned by the weight of Keith's charges or the potential embarrassment for her husband. Inevitably, speculation in the Canadian and world press suggested that Mrs Trudeau was having an affair with a Rolling Stone. A New York writer imagined that she had her eye on Ronnie Wood. There were staunch denials all round.

All the Stones but Keith flew to New York and Mr Trudeau publicly defended his wife, saying she had the right to a private life. However, he added that she had cancelled all forthcoming public engagements. By early April, Keith and Anita had joined the others in New York. The band played some gigs, discussed business, edited some live album tapes and attended more parties. Meanwhile, the brilliant American singer and guitarist Nils Lofgren, on tour in Britain, performed a new song dedicated to Keith Richard. 'Keith Don't Go (To Toronto)' seemed to say it all.

The cloud shadowed them all. Stories about Bianca's friendships with actor Warren Beatty and David Bowie didn't help. Charlie Watts went home to play jazz. Bill Wyman did the same, in Switzerland. Ronnie Wood sold his London home. And, while

maintaining that he wasn't a drug addict, Keith was undergoing detox in New York. Kind-hearted German fans launched an appeal to help him finance his tribulations. The band seemed to be in disarray. Their new album, *Love You Live*, was launched with a party in London in September, without Keith.

Recordings in Paris began almost immediately – but where were the songs, the cohesion, the energy? And where was Keith? Actually he made it to some of the sessions. In the context of punk rock, Mick said that Keith was the original: 'You can't really out-punk Keith.'

By this time, Mick had begun dating a tawny Texan model, Jerry Hall. She was clever and humorous, and her rangy beauty had earned her great success, so she was wealthy, too. She used to step out with Brian Ferry of Roxy Music, who did not like her new friendship.

In December 1977, the band stopped recording while Keith faced his trial at last. He was remanded to a higher court the following February. Mick and Jerry used the break to visit Morocco, later spending Christmas in London before flying to Barbados for New Year. Bianca was rumoured to be filing for divorce as the year ended, although she and Mick continued to deny the end of their marriage.

In early March 1978, Keith's trial in Canada was set for October. The suspense must have been almost unbearable. But in the meantime he was free to travel, record and perform. There were no long-distance tours this year. However, the Nanker/Phelge partnership blossomed anew as the Glimmer Twins co-wrote songs for the June-released *Some Girls* LP, the tracks 'Miss You' and 'Beast Of Burden' being among their finest. The album sleeve, which featured less-than-flatteringly adapted pictures of female film stars with portraits of Stones in wigs and make-up, caused another controversy.

More gigs – mainly in north America – stretched out this strained year. Mick celebrated his thirty-fifth birthday in California, after the last concert. No one seemed to ask him about his threat to retire at the age of thirty-three. Maybe everyone was just marking time to see what would happen to Keith. Interestingly, Mick had taken to playing guitar during the tour.

Bill and Charlie attended the London funeral of Keith Moon, the Who's drummer, on 7 September that year. Bill remarked a few days later that he was depressed and thinking of quitting.

On 23 October, almost two years after the original offence, Keith Richards' (he'd recently reinstated the final 's' to his name) trial began in Toronto. His efforts to

reform impressed the judge, and he escaped with a year's suspended prison sentence and an order to give a charity concert. He was also commanded to continue with his treatments for addiction. A packed court expressed relief and delight, and demand for the charity concert tickets was massive. Other factions were outraged by the judge's leniency and appealed against the light sentence. But Keith was effectively a free man, although it remained to be seen if the general cloud would lift.

Keith was in a dilemma, anyway. If he returned to Canada he could face a subpoena from lawyers who wanted the case reopened, but he'd be in breach of the court if he failed to turn up for the concert. The appeal was heard in June 1979 and, agonisingly again, the decision was reserved.

In October the previous year, Mick failed to receive Bianca's divorce papers because he was out of London. The documents were served the following April in New

York. Her lawyer was the celebrated 'palimony' expert, Marvin Mitchelson, who had already represented Marsha Hunt. Meanwhile Mick and Jerry Hall remained together. That Christmas he went to Hong Kong. Keith went to London to be with his family.

In January 1979 *Some Girls* was voted best album of the previous year by the *New Musical Express*. *Rolling Stone* had already given it a similar award and voted the Stones artists of the year. 'Miss You' was named best single. None the less, it is almost miraculous that the beleaguered band (with backing group the New Barbarians), managed to play several dates in north America that spring. Jagger had to discuss divorce strategies with his London lawyers. Those concerned may well have been alarmed by reports that Bianca wished to continue helping victims of the Nicaraguan civil war, but claimed she could do nothing without personal funds. Over a year passed before the divorce was finally heard in London in November 1979 – supposedly with neither happy at the eventual settlement. Bianca retained custody of nine-year-old Jade.

Perhaps we shouldn't pry too deeply for reasons for Mick and Bianca's failed marriage. Whatever happened in the past, Bianca would later remark that where Jade is concerned they will always remain united parents for her sake. Both rushed to their daughter's side from different continents when she was involved in a road accident in the Balearics in 2000.

Meanwhile Keith and Anita were in trouble again, this time in New York State. In August, a teenager watching TV in bed with Anita shot himself in the head with a stolen revolver. She was released on bail but her passport was confiscated. She said the boy had a death wish and she had taken pity on him, but that there was no sexual relationship. There were rumours, though, that she was involved with some kind of black magic.

In the face of all this, Keith's relief when the appeal against his life sentence was at last dismissed in recognition that he had kicked his drug addiction must have been enormous. He could get on with his work and life as a free man. Despite a weakening of ties to Anita, he must have been pleased when she was cleared of any involvement in the teenager's death, even though she was indicted on charges of illegal possession of a firearm.

As Christmas 1979 approached and another decade turned, Anita awaited sentence, Bill was again thought to be planning to leave the band and Charlie was playing jazz in small London clubs. Mick and Jerry were relatively untroubled.

CHAPTER TEN

Emotional Rescues

The Rolling Stones were more or less intact as the 1980s beckoned. But the axis of pop music had shifted yet again, with New Romantics and bands like ABC, Spandau Ballet and Soft Cell poised to carry the torch through this decade.

Even though the Rolling Stones had confounded critics, overcome personal troubles and survived to flaunt their 'trade-mark' of wide, slack lips on every piece of promotional material, the band may have struggled to remain both men of wealth and taste *and* ageing rebels. Words like 'veterans' and 'survivors' seemed unflattering and ageing. But more than one generation had grown up to a Rolling Stones soundtrack. The band were still rocking, and so were the fans.

Bill told the *Daily Express* in February 1980 that he would leave the Stones in September 1982, the band's twentieth anniversary, the year that Charlie would profess to hate rock 'n' roll and to disliking being a full-time Stone. Also in February 1980, Ronnie and new partner Jo

Howard were arrested for possession of cocaine. The charges were dropped when it was established that the drug had been planted. Could some of the Stones be considering a calmer way of life?

Increasingly, Bill and Charlie 'guested' on recordings and made appearances with jazz and blues musicians. They also scored music for mainstream films. But Mick remarked later in 1980 that he might remain a rock 'n' roller forever. The band's logo of those swollen lips with the sensuously lolling tongue had already become a design icon. The Stones, to some extent, had become a simple branded business – albeit a massive one.

Mick's interest in film seemed to be waning when he abandoned plans to star in Werner Herzog's (later celebrated) film *Fitzcarraldo*, and to produce and act in another film. He also declined a reportedly huge sum of money to appear in the American TV drama *Dallas*. His relationship with Jerry survived separations and stories about his affairs with actresses and models, and was to become one of rock 'n' roll's most enduring (and productive) unions: Elizabeth Scarlett, the first of their four children, was born in March 1984.

Keith seemed to remain the sole unreconstructed rocker. His relationship with Anita Pallenberg was over, and he married Patti Hansen, an American actress and model, on 18 December 1983 – his fortieth birthday. He remained a devoted father, which called for some stability

and responsibilities. However, he had remarked in 1981 that he'd be playing rock 'n' roll in a wheelchair – it was what he did for a living.

The band's 1981 single 'Start Me Up', cut from the *Tattoo You* LP, went to the UK No. 1 slot, and their 1982 tour had been their most successful ever. But as Mick and Keith approached their fortieth birthdays in 1983, incredulous and faintly patronising things were said and written about superannuated rock stars. Needless to say, the Stones were untroubled by this. And the facts spoke for themselves. During an American tour that year, the band filled venues with up to 90,000 capacity. Polls such as those among *Rolling Stone* readers kept voting them best band, Mick best vocalist and their albums best of the year.

It has been suggested that the energy Mick spent during any one performance was comparable to running twenty miles. Mindful perhaps of a landmark birthday, or simply being in reflective mode, he began a programme that included running, rowing and training in the martial arts. He also accepted a large amount of money to write his memoirs. These memoirs have never been completed or published, Mick famously claiming that he couldn't remember enough about the early years to tell the story. It was also said that Bill declined to assist because he was saving up the best bits for his own story. In May 1984, it was reported that Mick was considering returning his advance. Soon after, the wily Wyman was reputed to have trumped Jagger by signing an even bigger financial deal for his own diaries.

It was around this time that some members of the Stones became involved with fund-raising work. Bill and Charlie supported ARMS, the multiple sclerosis charity, and the band performed before the Prince and Princess of Wales at a Prince's Trust gala in September 1983. Then it was announced that Mick was sponsoring Britain's gymnasts for the 1984 Los Angeles Olympics, partly to acknowledge the value of his father's work as a PE teacher. Charlie played in Edinburgh to raise money for famine-blighted Ethiopia.

Yet still the band's power to outrage was undiminished. In November the BBC banned a video for their single 'Undercover Of The Night' for its depiction of a terrorist murder. Mick maintained that the film was a protest against totalitarian regimes. The song went to No. 11 in Britain before Christmas 1983 in spite of – possibly because of – these constraints.

In spring 1984, Bill was reported in the *Sun* newspaper as having made critical comments about two fellow band members. A week later he denied it. In the summer,

as Mick prepared for the release of his solo album *She's The Boss* (which was to enjoy modest chart success), he dismissed rumours that the band were disintegrating. He said that individual projects would not threaten the Stones' future and that there was enthusiastic planning rather than dissent.

Simultaneous London and Philadelphia Live Aid concerts took place in July 1985. Mick sang in the USA with Daryl Hall and John Oates, and then with Tina Turner. Ronnie and Keith joined Bob Dylan later, and Mick also dueted with David Bowie in a rendition of 'Dancing In The Street', which became a major hit single and video classic. It was a nice welcome to the world for James Leroy Augustine, Mick and Jerry's first son, who was born on 28 August.

But 1985 closed sadly, with the death in December of Ian Stewart. Ian had quietly been at the heart and spine of the Stones as driver, sometime pianist and wise friend since the start. The band played at a memorial gig for him in London in the new year.

Amid new rumours of a split, particularly of disagreements between Mick and Keith, the latest album, *Dirty Work*, made a more than respectable No. 3 in the UK charts in April 1986. But the Glimmer Twins did sometimes seem to arrange to be in separate cities, and

other members of the band were increasingly interested in solo directions – especially Charlie with his jazz orchestra. Some attention was diverted from this by sixteen year-old Mandy Smith's revelations about her affair with forty-nine year-old Bill. (They would eventually marry, but divorce soon afterwards. Both have remarried since – Mandy's second husband is a footballer only slightly older than her and Bill's bride in her thirties.)

Altogether, 1987 was not a vintage year for the Stones. In January 1988 Ronnie Wood opened a nightclub, Woody's, on Miami's soon-to-be ultra-cool South Beach. It was designed by Barbara Hulanicki, the genius behind Biba, who had settled there with her customary flair for knowing the right time for the right place. Sadly the club didn't stay open long because of complaints about noise.

The band may not have collected quite so many awards for being best something-or-other at the new year's music business polls. But this didn't break any hearts: tickets for Mick's forthcoming Japanese shows had been an instant sell-out.

By May 1988 there was something of an armistice when all five Rolling Stones convened for the first time in two years at a London hotel. They agreed that they would work together again, in the studio and on tour. *Rolling Stone* magazine would shortly announced that '(I Can't

Get No) Satisfaction' was the best single of the past twenty-five years, which may well have provided some motivation for the band to continue.

Mick had the separate satisfaction of seeing Jerry reprise the Marilyn Monroe role in a New Jersey stage production of the play *Bus Stop*. They celebrated his forty-fifth birthday on her first night. While still planning solo gigs, Mick and Keith met in New York to further discuss and strengthen the Stones' future. Mick also announced the following month (in Australia where he was touring), that he would retire when he was fifty.

In the autumn Keith, whose live solo gigs had been cheerful (if unremarkable) affairs, spoke to *Rolling Stone* about his relationship with Mick. He may well have alluded to Mick having a Peter Pan complex and controlling tendencies, but he also stressed that Mick had always stood by him as a faithful friend throughout the years. Finally, he confirmed that the Stones would soon be rocking together again.

The band would seem to be in harmony again. They talked of their joint future together in New York in 1989 and in meetings between combinations of two or three of them. Talk of reconciliation wasn't idle chit-chat. In March, the Stones signed rock's biggest-ever tour deal. They also gathered in Montserrat in May to record. Fifty-two year-old Bill managed to find time during the sessions to phone a marriage proposal to nineteen year-old Mandy.

She displayed her Asprey's engagement ring at the launch of Bill's new Kensington restaurant, Sticky Fingers, on 9 May. The restaurant still flourishes.

Wedding arrangements were so secret that even Bill's seventy-six year-old mother didn't know about them. Afterwards she said she was disappointed but not surprised, commenting that he had always been a rebel. A few days later the marriage was blessed in London before a party for four hundred guests.

Meanwhile the new album was mixed. But there were reports that Mick and Charlie were less than happy with each other after a group meeting in Amsterdam. Mick had apparently referred to Charlie as 'his drummer'. Charlie, quite reasonably, responded by referring to Mick as 'his singer'. The squabble seems to have resulted in someone landing face first in a plate of smoked salmon. Nonetheless, plans for the next American tour proceeded.

The tour began in the late summer, including concerts in Toronto, to promote a new album, *Steel Wheels*, and single, 'Mixed Emotions'. Almost twenty years after Altamont, some of the Hell's Angel fraternity still bore a grudge about comments Mick was reported to have made about them. He was therefore given round-the-clock security protection. Despite that, the *Steel Wheels* tour was a sell-out and it became clear that the restless spirit behind the Stones' boast to be the greatest rock 'n' roll band in the world was still as strong as ever.

EPILOGUE

Time Is On My Side

It seems that the Rolling Stones are much more than the sum of their parts. This is not to dismiss individual talents and separate enterprises. Far from it. Such solo expressions of great talent have served to strengthen the Stones as a band whenever they gather on stage or in the studio. So however marvellous private passions indulged may be, it is when the band collide and convene that the brilliance and magic returns.

Touring may well bring with it an element of repetition. But truthfully life on the road can't have been quite as tough as waiting in the rain morning after morning for a bus or enduring mindlessly repetitious office tasks. One can only conclude that they still enjoy the circus after all these decades and feuds. One can also hope that Mick Taylor, who managed to escape, is happier now.

Bill wasn't alone and broken-hearted for long after his marriage to Mandy ended. He married Suzanne Daccosta, a Californian fashion designer in her thirties, five months after the divorce. Then there was an even bigger upheaval – he left the Rolling Stones in January 1994. After all his hints over the years few were surprised. Bill had always been a little detached, on stage and off, and he hated flying. He seemed far happier running his restaurant and pursuing other private interests. After all this time – even after Brian's death, Mick Taylor's departure and the Glimmer Twins' tensions – there seemed to be something concrete about the body of the band. But now Bill has his own musical enterprises and business affairs, and the means to enjoy a comfortable retirement.

Mick and Jerry would also face and weather storms in the 1990s. Mick's womanising did not seem to perturb Jerry much, and after the birth of Elizabeth, three further children loudly made the point that all was well. Mick and Jerry had always had a tolerant and understanding relationship, and the couple even went through a marriage ceremony in 1990 in Indonesia. But towards the end of the decade Mick plucked one dusky beauty too many. In May 1998, when the twenty-nine year-old Brazilian model Luciana Morad gave birth to a son, Jerry's patience expired.

At first, Mick denied paternity. But DNA tests decided that he was the father and he committed to modest maintenance payments. Mick also disputed that Jerry and he were ever legally married. But despite their wrangles at the time, the two of them seem warmly amicable today, even comfortable together and determined that their children should not be victims in the parting. Mick supportively attended the West End first night of *The Graduate* in which Jerry was briefly required to strip naked in the role of the mature temptress Mrs Robinson.

Charlie and Shirley Watts have remained as stable as ever. Jo and Ronnie Wood also seem to have forged a rock-solid marriage. And Keith … well, Keith and Patti are still together and have a family. His heroin addiction appears to be a thing of the past and he looks (almost) astonishingly well.

And the music has continued. It's in the blood and certainly the most enduring of any of the Rolling Stones' collective addictions. Mick might have resumed his deep interest in movie projects – such as his company Jagged Films' production of the Robert Harris novel *Enigma* in 1999 – but this was of little consequence for the band. Even without Bill as corner Stone, even without Mick Taylor, and now with the memory of Brian distant indeed, even with Charlie Watts quietly diversifying and the extensive responsibilities of his jazz orchestra,

the band can still do the business like no other. Now that Ronnie Wood has long been regarded as a fully fledged Stone, not as some cheerfully obliging stand-in, and with Mick and Keith friends again and still craving to rave when other commitments don't intrude – or perhaps even because of them – the Stones have somehow managed to stick together during the last years of the twentieth century almost as never before.

And in the end it is the Stones on tour that defines their enduring, ever-refreshed energy. Touring is exhausting but it always, conversely, regenerates and pumps the blood back into the unstoppable machine that the Rolling Stones has become. It is in their collective breath, guts and blood.

It may be that band members privately yearn for the intimacy of small, smoky clubs and a short set of pure blues, but you won't find much public sentimentalising about the old days. The band still seem to relish the enormity of the productions, the stadiums, the ramps, spectacular lights and special effects that keep an entourage upwards of 100 people busy between shows, pre-show and back-stage. And the little luxuries of modern touring help to give the fans value for money over performances that can last hours and span thirty songs. As Charlie Watts has remarked, the days of staying in shabby bed and breakfast places were not much fun. Speaking of the band's ability to keep going, he says they couldn't have done it without the perks.

Keith reportedly said of *The Voodoo Lounge* tour, which began in 1994 and included the Stones' first Australian and New Zealand gigs for over twenty years that their performance improved every night and that the best show of the whole tour was probably the last gig at Wembley.

The *Bridges To Babylon* tour, which opened in Chicago in 1997 and lasted until the end of the millennium, featured (appropriately enough) a bridge flung across the world's auditoriums. It seemed to symbolise the band's ability to reach across generations, across time and into the hearts and hips of every single person throughout the world who'd bought a piece of the Rolling Stones experience for the price of a ticket. And it would be folly for anyone, especially a Stone, to predict when the band will stop rolling.

The two great mantras of the 1960s rock 'n' roll generation were 'Live fast, die young' and 'Hope I die before I get old'. But now there's another, ladies and gentlemen, as we continue to welcome the Rolling Stones, now and forever 'The Greatest Rock And Roll Band In The World'.

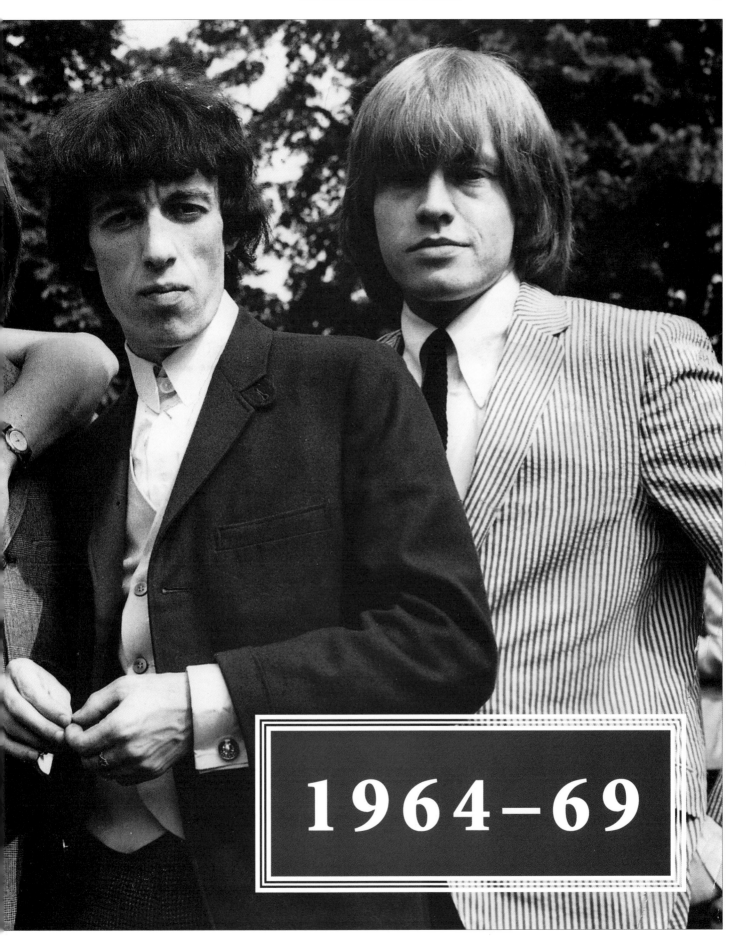

1964–69

Mick, Charlie, Brian, Bill and Keith

In early 1962 Mick Jagger and Keith Richards (*opposite*) meet by chance on a train and quickly become friends. Soon after they hear Brian Jones (*left*) play slide guitar at the Ealing Jazz Club, and a band is formed that will be the nucleus of the Rolling Stones. In July 1962 they play a gig at the Marquee in London, still under their previous name the Rollin' Stones.

By the beginning of the new year Charlie Watts (*above*) and Bill Wyman have joined Mick, Keith and Brian, and now the band is called the Rolling Stones. The band work hard during 1963 under the direction of Andrew Loog Oldham, their newly-acquired manager, playing in clubs and at parties until they are ready to cut their first single. 'Come On/ I Wanna Be Loved' was released in June 1963, reaching No. 20 in the charts.

Mick (*opposite*), Brian and Keith moved into a flat in Edith Grove, Chelsea together, although it was a struggle to pay the rent. However, by November 1963 they had released a second single, 'I Wanna be Your Man', which spent thirteen weeks in the UK charts, and it was beginning to look like the Rolling Stones had a future.

When Bill Wyman (*above*) joined the Stones he was already playing semi-professionally, although by day he worked as a storekeeper in South London.

Overleaf A rare early picture of the band.

Taking off

Left Mick and Keith in Carnaby Street in London. The band's first album, *The Rolling Stones,* is released and reaches No. 1 in the British album charts on 24 April.

Below The Stones at a London airport. April 1964 and the band is *en route* to the Montreux Television Festival in Switzerland.

Opposite The Stones at Montreux. By now the band is in high demand and they are invited to all kinds of media events.

Hotel hell in UK tour

By May of 1964 the band had embarked on their third UK tour. Failing to observe the dress code in a smart Bristol hotel, they were refused lunch. A few days later in Hamilton, Scotland, police had to restrain 4,000 fans who stormed a gig in a local hotel.

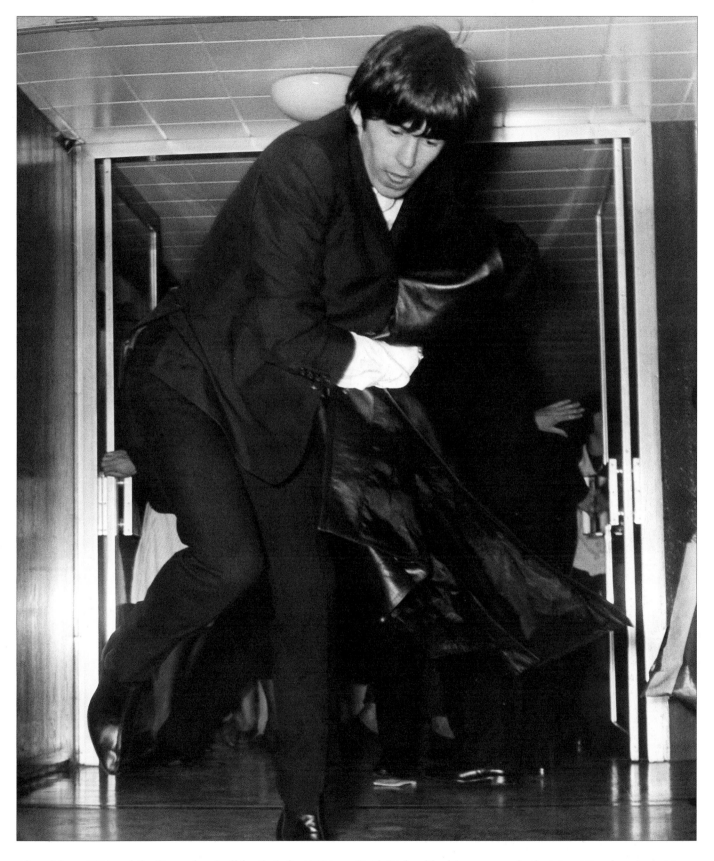

Above 1 June 1964 and the Stones head off for their first US tour. Keith Richard had to use some back stairs at London airport to elude a mob of girls who wanted to see them off. Only their manager, Andrew Loog Oldham, was confident that the tour would be a success. Their recent first US single, 'Not Fade Away', had not sold particularly well. After an uncertain start, the final two concerts of the tour at Carnegie Hall were both instant sell-outs.

'Papa Was A Rolling Stone'

Opposite Bill Wyman holds his two-year-old son Stephen before leaving for the three week US tour. His wife Diane, as ever, is discreetly in the background.

Right At a press conference on the band's return from the States on 23 June, the police had to cope with rioting fans who tried to gain entry.

Below The Stones, none of them particularly tall, helped to popularise footwear that became known as Chelsea boots. Brian Jones (*left*), and Keith Richard (*right*) share centre stage with Mick Jagger for a TV recording.

Jagger fined for speeding

Opposite Mick Jagger leaving a Liverpool court with his manager Eric Easton after being fined £32 for speeding in August 1964. Things were to look up a few days later though, as the band's EP 'Five by Five' hit the British singles chart.

Andrew Loog Oldham, who had been employed briefly by Brian Epstein to publicise bands, had seen the Rolling Stones play in Richmond. After Epstein turned down Oldham's proposal that they both managed the group, Oldham asked Easton to come and watch them. Soon after the band signed a management contract with Oldham and Easton.

Above When Charlie and Shirley married quietly in Yorkshire on 14 October 1964, not even the other Rolling Stones were told. The couple feared that their news would upset Charlie's fans.

Previous page The Rolling Stones receive an award for being most popular group at a Variety Club of Great Britain luncheon at London's Savoy Hotel in September 1964. Despite looking pensive, Brian Jones *(far right)*, grinned when asked how they felt about pipping the Beatles for the accolade.

A quiet wedding

Despite a very private ceremony, Shirley Watts epitomised the fashionable mid-sixties bride – blonde bob, boucle coat, yellow dress and strappy low-heeled shoes. Shirley was an art student – as Charlie had once been. She intended to teach after her marriage, but it's been thirty-eight years now and she hasn't started yet.

Opposite After a brief honeymoon, Shirley Watts had to wave farewell to Charlie as he left for the Stones' second US tour on 23 October.

On their return from the tour, Decca released 'Little Red Rooster', a blues song first recorded by Howlin' Wolf. Oldham had been reluctant to release it as a single, but the band, Charlie in particular, was keen. The record went straight to No. 1 in the UK charts.

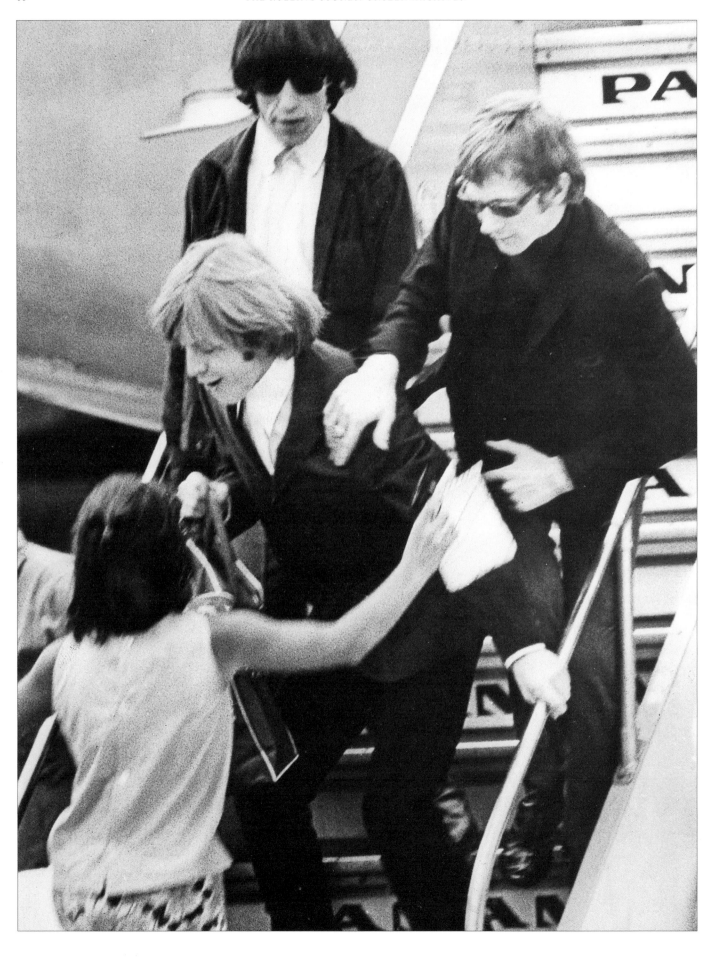

First Australian tour

Arriving at Sydney for their first Australian tour on 21 January 1965. Barricades broke and 3,000 fans burst through a police cordon. Here, manager Andrew Loog Oldham – in trade-mark shades – helps Brian Jones to ward off a particularly enthusiastic fan.

Below Mick on stage in 1965. By then the writing was on the wall for Mick Jagger's long-term girlfriend Chrissie Shrimpton – he'd fallen for Marianne Faithfull, an aristocratic blonde teenager whose first hit record, 'As Tears Go By', was written by Jagger and Keith Richard.

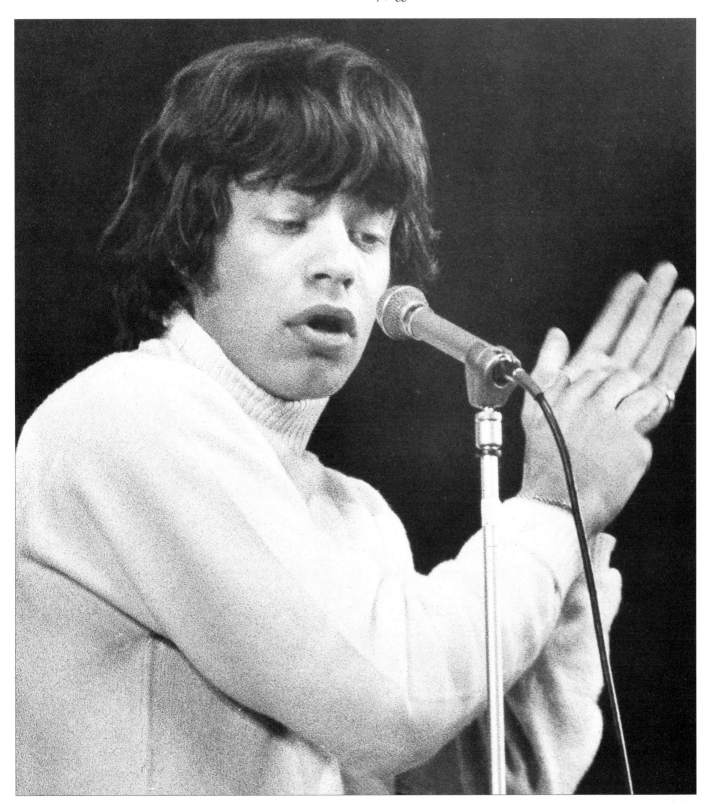

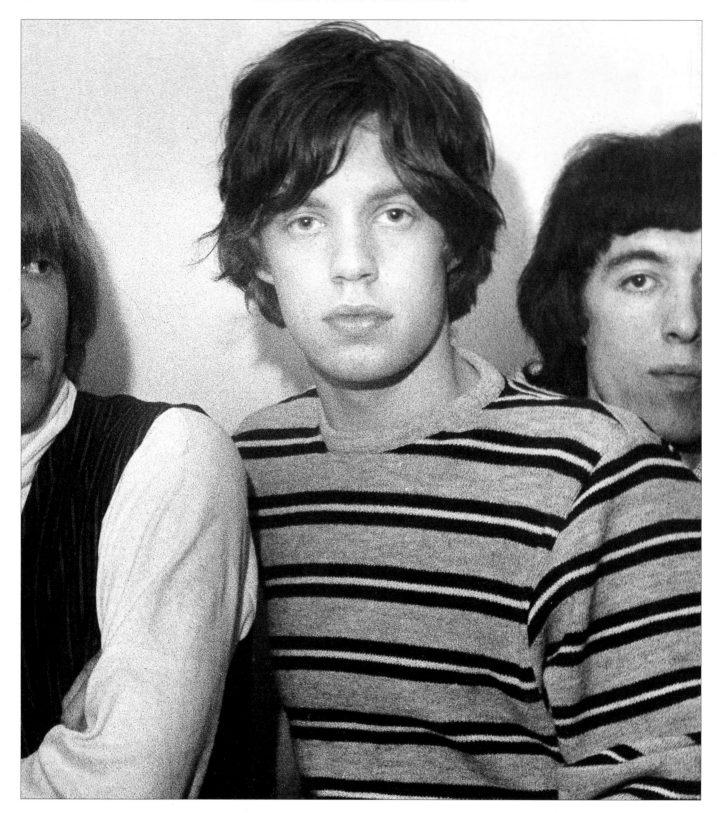

The leader of the Stones?

Mick, Brian and Bill on the Stones' third tour of North America in May 1965.

Opposite above Mick Jagger with rock legend James Brown. The Rolling Stones, most notably Keith Richard and

Charlie Watts, have never forgotten their debt to black American blues and jazz musicians.

Opposite below The band takes a moment while on a short tour of Scotland in June the same year. Rumours were rife that Brian and Mick didn't see eye to eye about who led the Stones.

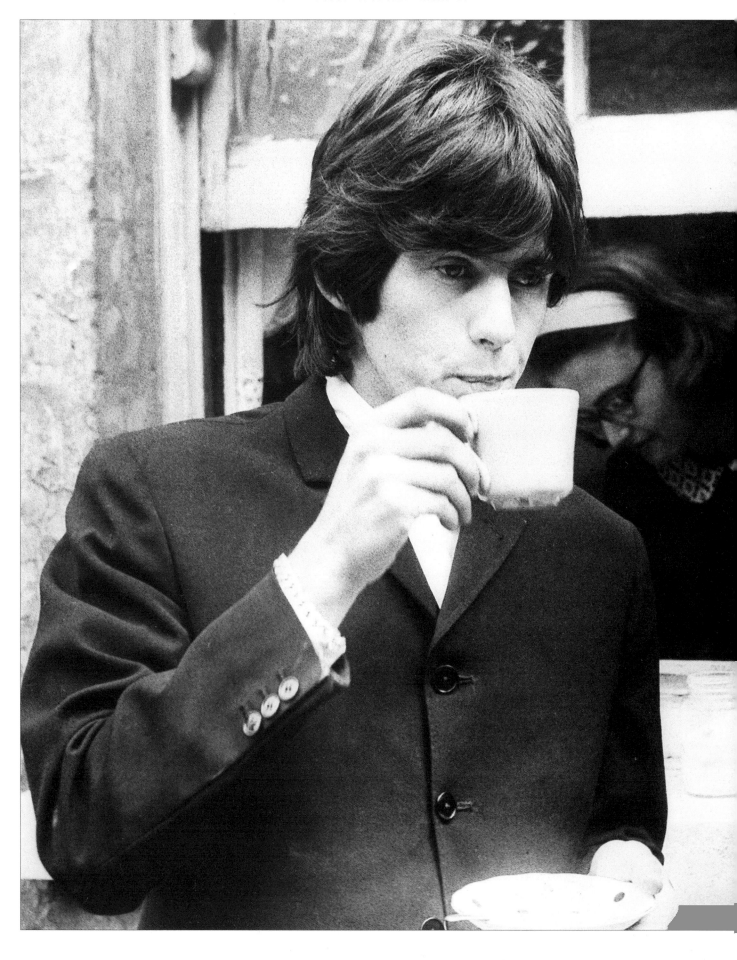

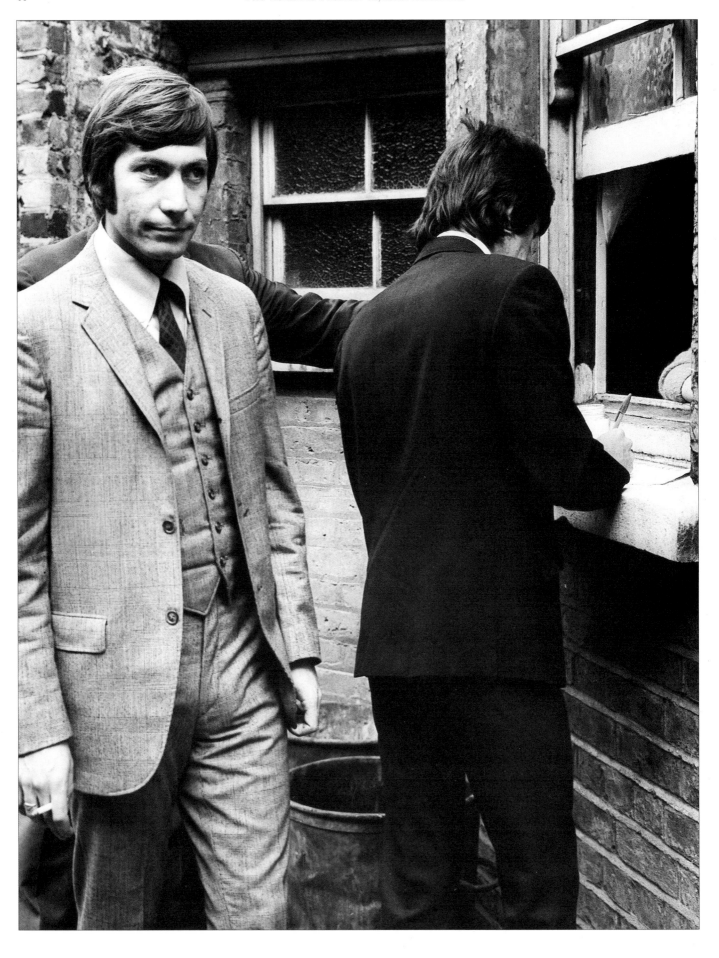

'Insulting behaviour'

Previous page Keith and Charlie take a break outside court.

Opposite A sharp-suited Charlie Watts and Keith Richard waiting outside a London magistrates' court in July 1965, where charges of 'insulting behaviour' relating to an incident in which they urinated on a garage forecourt are heard against the other three band members.

Above Bill Wyman, along with Brian Jones and Mick Jagger, was later fined £5.

In contrast to their attitude towards the Beatles, who had just been awarded MBEs, much of the press and many ordinary people were hostile to the Stones. It was not the police that brought the case to court, but the garage owner and a member of the public.

'Satisfaction' on tour

Previous page and opposite Messrs Jagger, Richard and Wyman appear to be unconcerned as police officers stand guard during a break in court proceedings relating to the garage incident. The case shocked parents and delighted Stones fans across the country.

Although the press concentrated on their misdemeanours, the band worked hard during 1965. The year began in Australia and the Far East, then there were various shorter tours of Britain and Europe. They also had spells in America in the spring and the autumn, and took time out to work in the recording studio. The chart-topping single 'Satisfaction' was originally recorded at the Chess Studios in Chicago and later reworked at the RCA studio where *Out Of Our Heads* was made.

Above Brian Jones with friend 'Betty' at Tangier airport in August 1965. She had pretended to be with the other man in the picture, but was actually accompanying Jones. Brian was fascinated by the colours, clothes, music and spirituality of Morocco and Marakesh. Soon he was to meet Anita Pallenberg and together they made several trips to North Africa.

Dating Chrissie Shrimpton

It was a special occasion, so Mick Jagger had his hair cut. He was best man at the London wedding of legendary French beauty and film star Catherine Deneuve and celebrated photographer David Bailey in August 1965. Bailey used to step out with Jean Shrimpton, the first supermodel, whose sister Chrissie was Mick's girlfriend.

Below Rioting fans, injuries and police discipline marred a Rolling Stones concert in Berlin in September 1965. Fifty rows of seats were demolished, and a train was vandalised. The band's popularity was undiminished though – in November that year, 'Get Off Of My Cloud' was No. 1 simultaneously in the UK and the USA.

Opposite On Christmas Eve 1965 Mick Jagger and Chrissie Shrimpton return from a holiday in Jamaica. They were to split soon afterwards, and Jagger began seeing Marianne Faithfull.

Overleaf The Stones on their travels again.

Seven weeks at No. 1

Left Bill Wyman – impassive, unsmiling and the corner Stone of a band now bathed in worldwide admiration. The classic album *Aftermath* was released in April 1966 and spent seven weeks at No. 1 in the British charts.

While their previous album *Out Of Our Heads* only contained four Jagger and Richard compositions, all fourteen of the tracks on *Aftermath* were their own. In 1966 Mick and Keith had also written Cliff Richard's single 'Blue Turns To Grey' and Chris Farlowe released 'Out Of Time', a track from *Aftermath*.

Above Keith Richard at the London premiere of Roman Polanski's cult film *Cul de Sac*. His companion was Mari Ann Moller, but no deep romance ensued.

Mick and Chrissie split

Chrissie and Mick in February 1966 – this time they are off to New York, where the group is doing some TV appearances.

Chrissie's relationship with Mick ended in December 1966. Both their stricken faces in these photographs suggest that things were not going well.

Fifth American tour

Previous page A rarely seen glimpse of the Rolling Stones without Mick Jagger, and a smiling Brian and Charlie in New York, 1966. The band's fifth American tour began in June that year. So many hotels had refused to take their booking that on arrival in New York they stayed on a yacht moored in the harbour.

Opposite By January 1967 Mick Jagger could sit, almost enthroned, knowing that his band had conquered the world. A new single, 'Let's Spend The Night Together' had just been released, shortly followed by an album, *Between The Buttons*. He also now had Marianne Faithfull on his arm.

When on the *Ed Sullivan Show* in America, the Stones were forced to change the title of the single to 'Let's Spend Some Time Together'.

Above Mick Jagger shortly before being banned from appearing on Eamonn Andrews' TV show because the band planned to sing to a pre-recorded backing track. Soon it would become routine for pop stars to mime – even to hit songs that had been recorded by session musicians – but it caused controversy at the time.

'Let's Spend the Night Together'

Opposite A compromise with the show's producers seemed to be reached when the band played 'She Smiled Sweetly' which they could do live, instead of their current smash, 'Let's Spend The Night Together'.

Above 23 February 1967, and a luminously beautiful Marianne Faithfull and smartly dressed Mick Jagger upstage Covent Garden patron Princess Margaret by arriving at the Royal Opera House five minutes late. Sticklers for protocol were outraged.

Drugs charges

Opposite Keith Richard travelling between London and Paris. A series of drugs-related charges clouded his and Mick Jagger's lives that summer. In February the police raided Redlands, Richard's Sussex home. Amongst other evidence, they took away amphetamines found in the pocket of a jacket belonging to Marianne Faithfull. Jagger claimed that the jacket and the drugs were his.

Left and below Work or pleasure? Mick leaves London for some of both in Paris in April 1967. The Stones' three week European tour had just finished.

Band on the brink

Opposite Mick Jagger in May 1967. The Stones had just completed a European tour, during which relations between the band and the police and customs officials had been tense, given the band's association with crowd violence and alleged drugs offences. On 10 May Jagger and Richard appeared in court following the raid on Richard's home.

Above A band on the brink. Some eyes meet the camera, others don't. Only the two 'quiet men' at the back seem able to meet the lens. Brian Jones had also been arrested for separate drugs-related offences the same day, and he, Jagger and Richard were all out on bail.

Trials and tribulations

Above Adoring girl fans can't begin to lift Keith's mood as he faces the first stage of the court proceedings that followed the recent drug bust at his Sussex home. It was alleged that a cocktail of drugs including marijuana and heroin were found during a party. Jagger was charged with possession, while Richard was accused of allowing the premises to be used for the smoking of Indian hemp. A friend of theirs, Robert Fraser, was charged with possession of heroin and amphetamines.

Opposite Bill Wyman's interest in charitable work began early. Here he holds the hand of his five-year-old son Stephen as they attend the opening of a community association retreat in Essex during May 1967.

Bill Wyman and Charlie Watts were not involved in any of the court cases and were encouraged by Jagger to begin work on a new Stones album in response to the Beatles' *Sgt Pepper's Lonely Hearts Club*. The album, which had been long-awaited by fans, was eventually titled *Their Satanic Majesties Request*. Although advance orders were worth $2,000,000 in the US, the album was not a critical success.

Jones convicted

Brian Jones at his own court proceedings following his arrest at home in Kensington in May 1967 for possession. He was soon to face a jail sentence, but this was commuted on appeal on the grounds of his fragile health – he spent time in hospital because of nervous strain.

Below Keith Richard outside the Chichester court. The court heard the cases against Mick Jagger and Robert Fraser first but did not sentence either of them until after Keith's case had been dealt with. As a result Jagger and Fraser spent time in Lewes prison until the court was ready to sentence all three.

Opposite Mick's smile is as wide as his trendy tie, but Keith faced the more serious charge and looks understandably glum.

Chichester courthouse

Above Mick and Keith at Keith's house Redlands, before their next appearance at Chichester court for their trial on 27 June 1967.

Opposite Mick and Keith outside the courtroom. When they adjourned for lunch, police had to clear a way as they were mobbed by hundreds of screaming teenagers.

Jagger jailed in Brixton

Opposite above Keith and Mick about to receive the verdict. Mick raised a tight smile, but Keith could only frown as reality loomed. If found guilty, he could face a maximum sentence of ten years in prison.

Opposite below Keith leaves a Chichester hotel after lunch with his lawyer. On his return to court he received a jail sentence of one year; Mick was sentenced to three months.

Above On 29 June 1967 Mick Jagger, Keith Richard and Robert Fraser were driven to prison to begin their sentences. Jagger was taken to Brixton, but Richard and Fraser were sent to Wormwood Scrubs.

Free men

Previous page The strain shows on the faces of Mick and Keith even as they are driven to London in a Bentley on 30 June 1967 following their release from prison on bail, pending appeals against their convictions. A broad public outcry had greeted the severity of their sentencing – even a *Times* editorial had criticised it.

Opposite and above Mick and Keith enjoy a drink in a pub near Fleet Street, London, on the day of their release. Mick had written poetry in prison. Keith admitted to weeping. The pair would have to wait weeks for their appeals to be heard, and were not allowed to leave the country in the meantime.

Mick's conditional discharge

Previous page Keith reviews recent events with companions. Mick seems pensive following his release from prison. The appeal was brought forward to 31 July. Keith had chickenpox and was not admitted to the courtroom for fear that the virus would be contagious. However, the news of the verdict, when it reached him, was good. Mick's sentence was altered to a one-year conditional discharge and Keith's conviction was quashed.

Above and opposite Later that day, having changed from formal attire into purple trousers and an embroidered jacket, Mick left London in a chartered helicopter with girlfriend Marianne Faithfull.

Destination unknown

Above and opposite No one knew where Mick and Marianne were headed but two weeks later, on 14 August, they arrived back from Ireland. Such was their noteriety, at Heathrow several taxi drivers refused to take them before one cabbie took pity on them. After the court case Mick and Marianne moved into 48 Cheyne Walk with her son Nicholas.

Left Brian Jones' case relating to drugs charges was finally heard. He was later sentenced to nine months in prison, commuted to three years' probation on appeal. Brian's mental state was fragile and one of the conditions of probation was that he should undergo psychiatric treatment.

Off again

September 1967 and Mick Jagger looks happy again as he makes his way to New York. When he and the other band members arrived they were questioned by immigration officials – there were fears that his earlier drugs conviction would prevent entry to the United States.

Right Brian heads off to New York on 13 September 1967. The pair embody his 'n' hers hippie chic.

Overleaf Wembley Arena, 12 May 1968 and the Stones are back in full cry with a surprise appearance at an annual concert sponsored by the NME. Brian Jones seems to have recovered from another spell in hospital for strain and exhaustion.

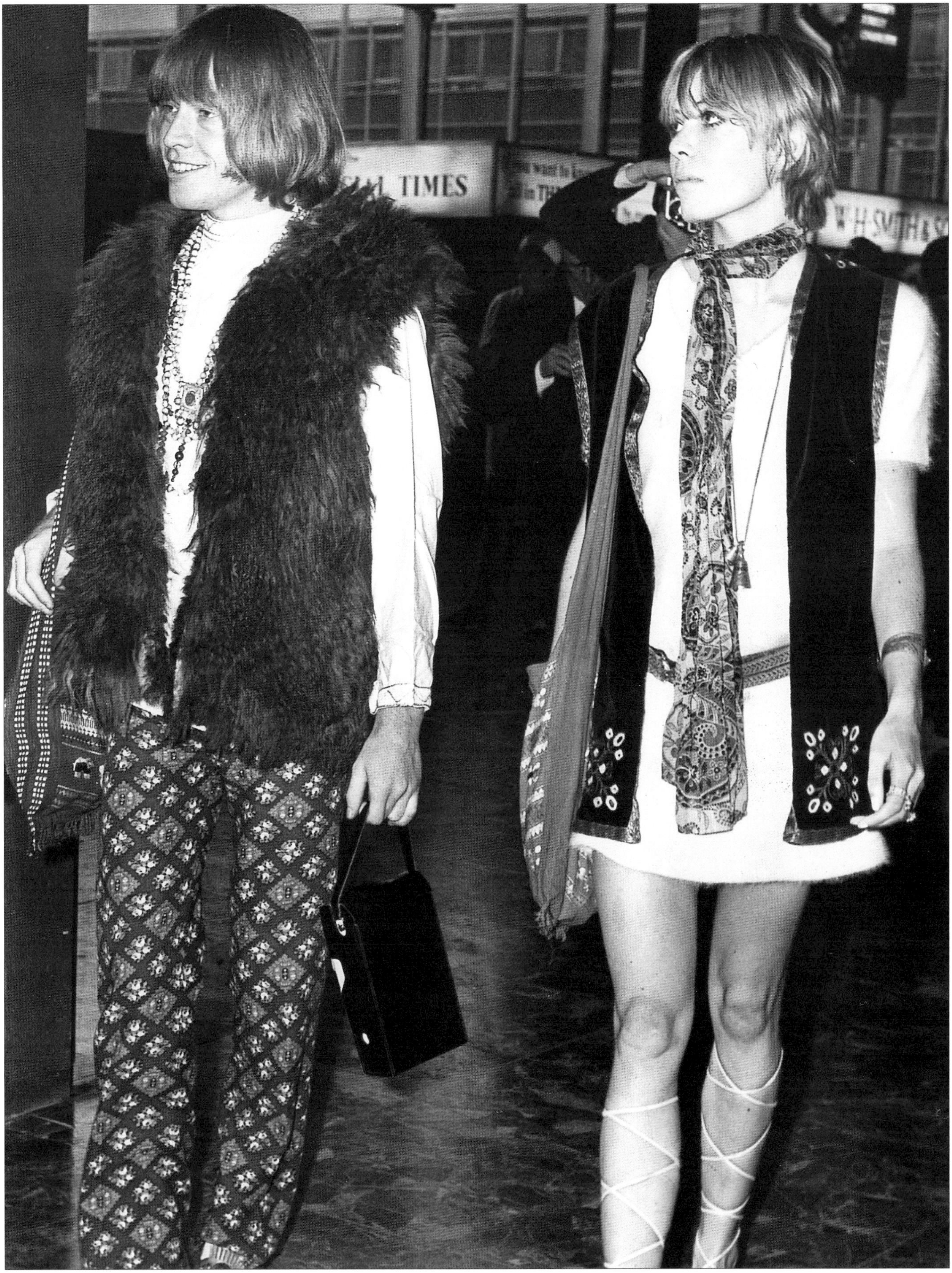
TIMES
W H SMITH

'Jumpin' Jack Flash'

Above Front man Mick gives his most gleeful crouching best at the NME gig as Keith and Brian are wired up behind.

The band performed 'Jumpin' Jack Flash' for the first time – it was released as a single two weeks later and reached No. 1 in the UK and the USA.

Performance

Above Mick Jagger with actor James Fox on 17 September 1968, on the set of the cult movie *Performance* in which Jagger's character wore women's make-up.

Opposite above Charlie and his wife Shirley assess the form. Shirley had given birth to a daughter, Serafina, on 18 March.

Opposite below Keith Richard and Anita Pallenberg on 18 July 1968 at the premiere of the Beatles' animated film *Yellow Submarine*. Richard and Pallenberg began seeing each other in March 1967 while her then boyfriend Brian Jones was in hospital in France with respiratory problems. Pallenberg played Mick's girlfriend in *Performance* and this led to tension between Keith and Mick.

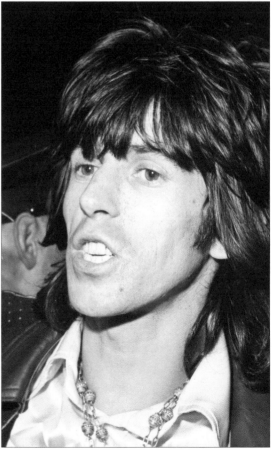

Jones back in court

Opposite above Brian Jones, pictured here on 26 September 1968 with his girlfriend Suki Poitier and tour manager Tom Keylock, reflects on a narrow escape: he had just been fined £50 for his second drugs offence. Although smartly suited for his court appearance his hair remains unrepentantly luxuriant. In an attempt to escape, Jones bought Cotchford Farm in Sussex two months later.

Opposite left Mick Jagger on the other hand submits to a savage hairstyle for his role in *Performance*.

Opposite right On Keith Richard's 25th birthday on 18 December, he, Anita Pallenberg, Mick Jagger and Marianne Faithfull flew to Brazil to discuss black and white magic with a mystic.

Rock and Roll Circus

On 5 December 1968 Mick and Marianne go to see the musical *Hair* in London, their first public outing since Marianne miscarried the previous month, six months into her pregnancy.

Opposite Five days later Brian is pictured with John Lennon, son Julian and Yoko Ono. Lennon planned to guest in the Stones' TV spectacular, *Rock and Roll Circus*. Much was made of the supposed rivalry between the Beatles and the Stones, but in reality they were great friends and supporters of each other. In fact both Mick and Keith had sung backing vocals on the Beatles' 1967 anthem 'All You Need Is Love'.

Jones set to leave

Mick and Marianne are arrested at their home in Chelsea on 28 May 1969. They are charged with drug-related offences but are released on bail and drive home. Mick maintains that the 'substances' being consumed at the time of the police raid were cherries, toast and honey.

Opposite and overleaf above Mick and Marianne outside Marlborough Street Magistrates Court in London on 29 May 1969 after hearing the charges relating to their alleged possession of cannabis. They were remanded on bail until 23 June.

But this was not the only thing on Mick's mind. The relationship between Brian Jones and the others was strained and everyone knew that action had to be taken. In May, Mick, Keith and Charlie drove to Cotchford to discuss the future and it was agreed that Brian should leave the band in exchange for a financial settlement.

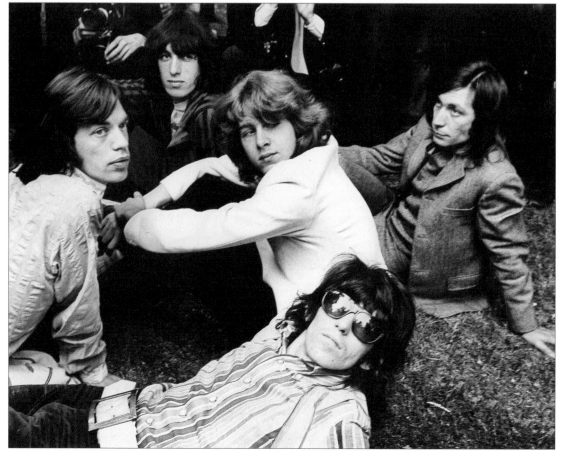

Mick Taylor joins the band

Left On 8 June Brian Jones leaves the Rolling Stones – musical differences are cited as the reason. Two days later twenty year old Mick Taylor, previously a guitarist in John Mayall's legendary Bluesbreakers, is recruited to replace Jones. He is pictured here in the centre, wearing a white shirt.

Opposite Mick and Marianne dress more formally for their court appearance on 23 June.

A new Stone

British audiences were to get their first look at new Stone Mick Taylor at a concert in July 1969 but American fans would see the new line up first when they recorded a US TV show at the end of June.

Death of a Rolling Stone

Brian Jones drowned in his Sussex swimming pool on the night of 2 July 1969. The band had already planned a free concert to celebrate their re-formation for 5 July and decided to proceed with it. Inevitably it became an emotional memorial to Brian and remains one of rock 'n' roll's seminal occasions.

Opposite Rolling Stones tour manager Tom Keylock stands outside Cotchford Farm, where Brian Jones had lived and died. The house had once been the home of A.A. Milne, who wrote the *Winnie the Pooh* stories there. Brian had been living and working there quietly as he planned his future.

Troubled times

Brian Jones was buried in his home town of Cheltenham on 10 July 1969. Shirley and Charlie Watts attended along with all the other Stones, except Mick Jagger who was filming in Australia, and had to cope with Marianne overdosing and falling into a coma. Only the day before, Bill Wyman (*left*), had been granted a divorce from his wife Diane and given custody of their son Stephen. During the proceedings it emerged that Bill was thirty-two – five years older than had been generally assumed.

'Please don't judge me too harshly'

At the funeral service the priest read from a telegram Brian had sent to his parents after a recent brush with the law saying, 'Please don't judge me too harshly.' In the Cheltenham streets where fans gathered, in the packed church and at the graveside, there were only expressions of affection and sorrow.

Left Shirley and Charlie Watts, she in the white mourning of eastern cultures, he in traditional black.

Below Mick and Marianne were unable to attend the funeral but sent flowers.

Opposite A recently divorced Bill with a female friend.

Mick plays Ned Kelly

Opposite Keith Richard, Anita Pallenberg and their baby son Marlon, born at King's College Hospital in London, on 10 August 1969. People often asked the couple about marriage plans and although there was to be a period when this seemed necessary due to Anita's 'alien' status in Britain, they never married. Long separated now, they remain friends nonetheless.

Above October 1969, Mick is pictured *en route* for recording in Los Angeles followed by their first American tour for three years. He had all but finished work on *Ned Kelly*. The reasons for going on tour were mainly financial. Most of the tour was organised in the UK – Ike and Tina Turner and B.B. King were booked as the supporting acts.

Final tour of the 1960s

Opposite December 1969, Keith and Charlie fly back after the dramatic and tragic concert at Altamont, California, during which three fans died and hundreds were injured. The concert had been policed by Hell's Angels, who took the law into their own hands when the crowd became restless.

Above Charlie is reunited with Shirley and daughter Serafina.

Left Keith is greeted by Anita and four-month-old Marlon. The couple field yet further enquiries about wedding plans.

Let It Bleed

Keith and Anita relax at home on 8 December 1969. They lived at 3 Cheyne Walk, a few doors down from Mick Jagger at number 48. Although often deemed to have an awesomely unhealthy lifestyle, Keith became a keen and competent skier under Anita's tutelage and the family made a home in Switzerland for some years.

Opposite 14 December 1969, and just back from California, the Stones (minus Bill Wyman) pose before a concert at the Saville Theatre in London. *Let It Bleed* was released in December 1969 and was the last album to be recorded on the Decca label.

Mick and Marianne plead 'not guilty'

Opposite Mick Jagger pictured on 19 December 1969 with Marianne Faithfull outside a London court where they pleaded not guilty to charges of possessing cannabis resin.

Above and Left The Rolling Stones in rehearsal at the Saville Theatre.

Playing out the decade

Previous page Mick and Marianne's court appearance on 19 December 1969 was to be the fourth time their case was heard. Two days later, Jagger and the band were scheduled to perform their Christmas party show at the Lyceum, London.

Opposite Marianne wore a long fur coat, almost as much for protection from more than a hundred photographers outside the London court as for warmth on this December day. Mick shields her from the crush.

Above On stage at the Lyceum on 21 December.

So long, Marianne

The trial had taken its toll and the couple had briefly separated,
during which time Marianne became involved with an Italian film
director. She returned to London but the relationship with Mick
was nearly over. Marianne was increasingly using drugs and Mick
did not spend much time at home. In the summer of 1970 she left
their house in Cheyne Walk and went to stay with her mother. Mick
had a number of relationships, but the most significant was with
the actress Marsha Hunt with whom he had a daughter, Karis.

Opposite On 31 May 1970 Jagger (*far left*), and
two other actors pose in Australian policemens'
uniforms in a publicity shot for his forthcoming
film about the outlaw Ned Kelly. The film was
directed by Tony Richardson and premiered in
London, but was not well received.

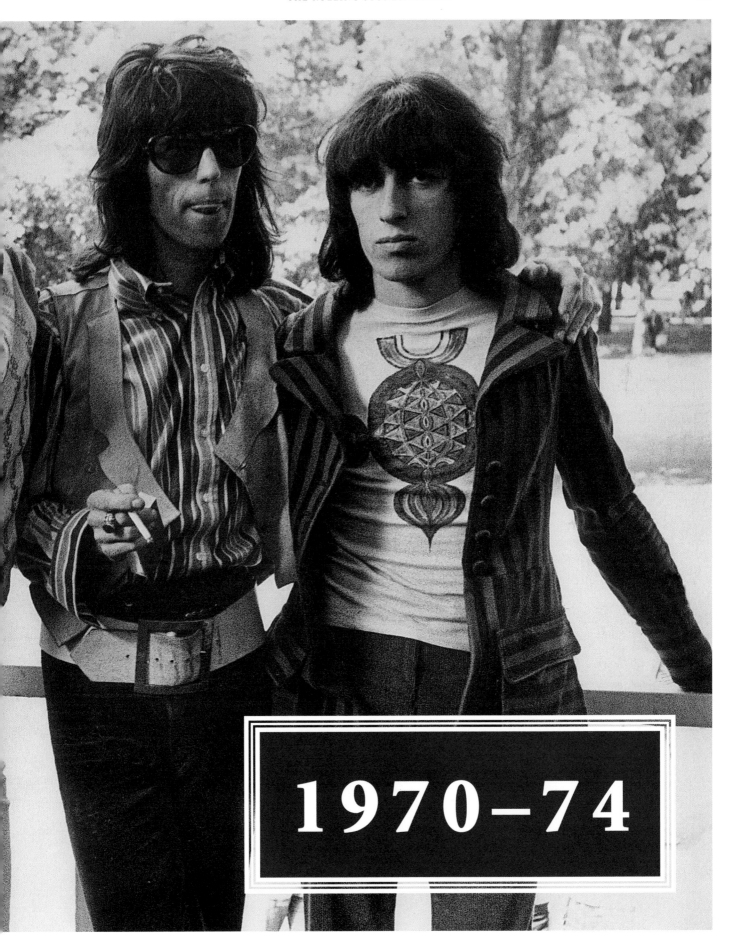

1970-74

New record deal

Opposite Off to the beach? No, Mick Jagger waits for his flight to Sweden, where the band is touring, on 1 September 1970.

At the end of July 1970 the Stones' recording contract with Decca had come to an end. They decided to sign a deal with Atlantic records allowing them to release albums on their own Rolling Stones label.

Left Mick Jagger stands back and allows Mick Taylor to take centre stage in Hamburg on 15 September 1970.

Above Mick, Mick and Charlie in Paris. Rolling Stones fans had running fights with French police. Some fans had tried to crash the first of three Paris concerts without tickets.

Playing Paris

The Stones on stage in Paris on 23 September 1970. Five thousand fans enjoy the show at the Palais des Sports. The day before the European tour ends, Mick is spotted in London with a new girlfriend, Nicaraguan Bianca Perez Morena de Macia, whom he had met in Paris.

Opposite Bill Wyman, his son Stephen and new girlfriend Astrid Lundstrom head for Astrid's native Sweden for a skiing holiday on 31 December 1970.

Exiles On Main Street

Early in 1971 it was announced that the Stones were set to leave London and base themselves in France. They began a 'farewell to Britain tour' with a show in Newcastle on 4 March 1971 and ended it with a concert at the Roundhouse in London.

Above Bill, Charlie and Astrid Lundstrom before the Newcastle concert. The Stones denied that leaving Britain for France had anything to do with tax breaks, but they made use of the 90 days each year they were allowed to spend in Britain.

Opposite Mick Jagger on 17 May 1971. He had just married Bianca on 12 May in a civil ceremony in St Tropez. Both wore white suits for the wedding, and the bride was several months pregnant. The marriage was almost cancelled because the press, who were legally entitled to attend the ceremony, refused to leave the building. The witnesses were Roger Vadim and Nathalie Delon. At the religious ceremony, held later in the day, Lord Lichfield gave away the bride. A daughter, Jade, was born in Paris on 21 October and Mick commuted back and forth from the south of France where the band was recording the *Exiles On Main Street* album.

Warm beer and cricket

It wasn't long before Mick was back in the country. During an interview on 11 May 1971 he spoke of the likelihood of pursuing solo musical projects as well as film work. However, an enduring love affair with France and many things French deepened during his time there and he now owns a chateau in the Loire valley. Just a small one, he assures us.

Opposite Bill Wyman and Astrid head off for a break in California on 24 May 1972.

Below Mick enjoys the warm beer (and indeed the dress code) of an English cricket match on 11 August 1972. His passion for cricket was sometimes dismissed as a pose but no one could deny it is real now. He is often seen at Lords, at the Oval, and at Test matches in the West Indies.

Mick: "I'll quit at 33"

Above Mick Jagger and friend at the Oval Test on 12 August 1972. Jagger announced a few days before that he intended to quit rock 'n' roll when he was 33.

Left Bill Wyman arrives back from the West Indies on 14 December 1972 after four weeks of recording at the Dynamic Sound Studios in Kingston, Jamaica. The band's interest in reggae music, just beginning to emerge, coupled with a desire to record in a technically advanced studio had attracted them there. *Goats Head Soup* was the resulting album.

Opposite Mr and Mrs Jagger arrive at a charity fashion gala at London's Savoy Hotel in January 1973. They had recently returned from Bianca's native Nicaragua, where they had been helping with the relief effort after a devastating earthquake.

Keith arrested

On 27 June 1973 Keith, Anita and a friend were in a London court on drugs charges, having been arrested the previous day. Keith was also charged with possession of a firearm and ammunition without a licence. They were released on £1,000 bail apiece.

Opposite Keith Richard on 1 August 1973. After their court appearance Keith and Anita, accompanied by their children Marlon and Dandelion, had returned to Redlands, their Sussex home. During the night a fire caused serious damage to the house.

'Angie' charts

Above Mick Jagger tilts his best side for the camera in Vienna on 3 September 1973. The band had just begun a two month European tour, starting in Mannheim and finishing in Berlin. 'Angie', a return to the type of ballad that the Stones had not recorded since the early days, entered the UK singles chart at No. 2 in August, and both the single and *Goats Head Soup*, the album it came from, would be No. 1 in the USA in October 1973.

On stage in Vienna

In 1973 the Stones had returned to Britain and tickets for the UK tour were an almost instant sell-out. More dates were hurriedly arranged.

Above Mick Jagger on stage in Vienna in September 1973. The tour reached Wembley on 7 September – one of four dates there.

Opposite Mick and Bianca could not have looked happier or better matched at the party they threw at Blenheim Palace on 7 September 1973. It confounded scandalmongers who had been linking Bianca with actors Ryan O'Neill and Elliot Gould, but there was still speculation as to why she did not accompany Mick on tour.

Proud Dad

Keith Richard spends some quality time with his children in September 1973. A month later, after the end of the European tour, he was charged with possession of various drugs, firearms and ammunition.

Rocking Wembley

Among the audience at the first Stones show at Wembley on 7 September 1973 were M*A*S*H stars Donald Sutherland and Elliot Gould (the latter rumoured to be sweet on Bianca Jagger). Ryan O'Neill was also there, as were hundreds of would-be gatecrashers who attempted to gain entrance to the sell-out gig by mingling with the 10,000 ticket-holding fans. A leather-clad Mick Jagger worked the crowd into a frenzy to the consternation of some pundits who, even then, were beginning to suggest that the Stones were too old to be rock 'n' roll stars.

Hitting the heights

Opposite and above The band on stage during the same series of Wembley shows. At the time the Rolling Stones were No. 1 in the album charts.

Moral support for Keith

Opposite Bill Wyman's impassive stage demeanour and subtly brilliant base licks also helped to keep the band focused on stage. Wyman was also beginning to think about working on his solo album *Monkey Grip* which was recorded in Los Angeles in January 1974.

Above Mick Jagger, just round the corner from Marlborough Street Magistrates' Court where he went to lend moral support to Keith Richard, who was fined £205 for possession of heroin and cannabis. Anita Pallenberg, who had been found in possession of Mandrax, was conditionally discharged.

Wood set to replace Taylor

Opposite Mick on stage in August 1974.

Above At the end of 1974 Mick Taylor decided that it was time to leave the band. Ronnie Wood, who had occasionally jammed with Keith during the previous year, was considered as a candidate to replace Taylor. However, Wood said that he was committed to the Faces.

Left A rare picture of Mick Jagger holding a guitar, 6 May 1974. Mick was already considering solo ventures, but it was another 10 years or more before he released his first solo single.

Fancy dress

Above Jagger in full spandex and rhinestone regalia, May 1974.

Opposite and overleaf Ronnie Wood at his south London home. Despite remaining with The Faces, Ronnie often hung out with Keith and the boys.

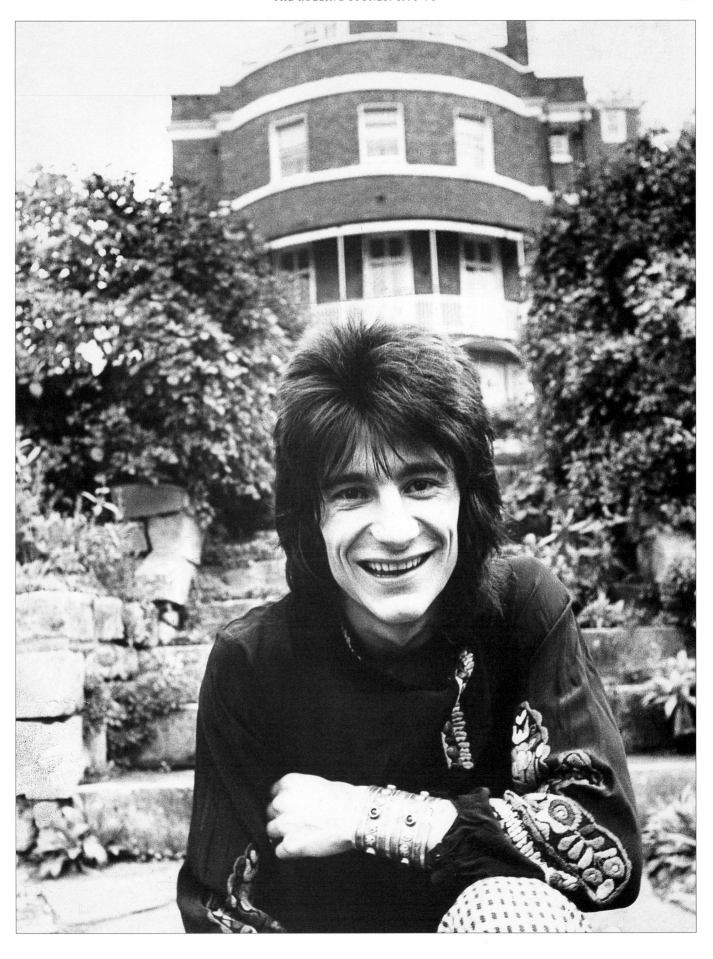

1975–79

Ronnie Wood 'on loan' from the Faces

Above Ronnie Wood with wife Krissie. Ronnie was a member of the Faces, and a friend of Keith Richard. When Mick Taylor announced he was leaving the Stones in December 1974 just as the band were about to leave for Munich to start work on a new album, Wood was touted as his successor. Various guitarists worked on the album, to be entitled *Black And Blue*, including Wayne Perkins and Harvey Mandel, as well as Ronnie Wood.

Opposite Ronnie Wood joined Jagger and other musicians in LA in March 1975 to jam, then went back to Munich to finish *Black And Blue*. In April he joined the Stones' American tour 'on loan' from the Faces, but had to leave part way through in order to re-join the Faces whose tour overlapped with that of the Stones. Rod Stewart was to quit the Faces in 1975, apparently unhappy with the Stones frequent 'borrowing' of Ronnie.

'How come you taste so good?'

Opposite Mick Jagger strikes a classic pose on stage in Cleveland, Ohio in June 1975, where the Stones played to more than 82,000 fans. The American tour began in New York when the band sang 'Brown Sugar' on the back of a truck travelling along Fifth Avenue.

Above Later that month Mick says his larynx is becoming strained and observers note him resorting occasionally to nips from a medicinal Jack Daniels bottle resting on a stage amp.

Disciple of Dirt

A crucifix may dangle across his naked chest, but Mick was dubbed 'Disciple of Dirt' by scandalised newspapers and parents across America during their 1975 tour. One paper deplored the Stones' 'demonic influence'. During the Baton Rouge shows in June outrage was particularly strong when a massive inflated phallus took centre stage as Mick sang 'Starf*cker'.

In July Keith and Ronnie were arrested in Arkansas and charged with carrying an offensive weapon. They were released on bail and later explained that the weapon was a tin-opener with an attached blade.

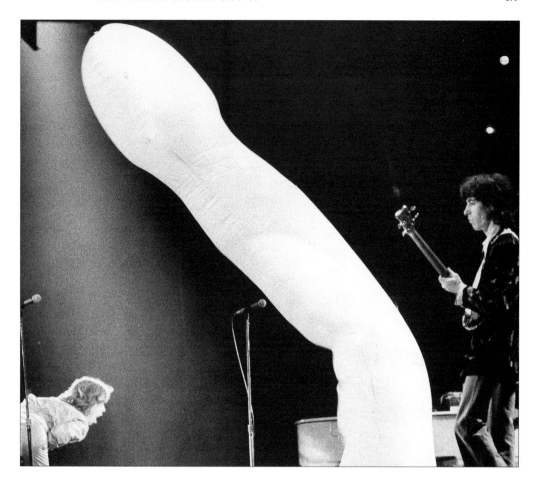

Longest tour

Keith wears an appropriate and unbuttoned Confederate-style shirt in Baton Rouge and looks more relaxed than Mick has at times on tour.

Opposite Mick Jagger in Baton Rouge, Louisiana, in June 1975. Time is still on his side during this longest-ever Rolling Stones tour of the Americas, but the lines are drawn – especially around the eyes. The tour finally finished in Buffalo in August, but they had planned it to be even longer – a number of shows in South America were cancelled in the end.

'I wish everyone was as happy'

Bill Wyman, Fellow of the Royal Horticultural Society, among the hothouse blooms at Kew Gardens in 1976. His interest in botany started when the Stones first toured in exotic places and he'd photograph the local plant life when he had time off. Despite the long face, he said in a newspaper interview in March that year 'I'm content with my career, my family, my hobbies. I wish everyone was as happy as me.'

One million apply for tickets

Left and opposite The Kings of Rock 'n' Roll at Earls Court in May 1976. A million people applied for tickets to the six London shows, the first in the capital for three years but only 100,000 fans were lucky enough to get in. The British tour cost over £1 million pounds to produce, thanks in part to stage props such as an 80 ft silk dragon that was suspended over the audience.

Above Bill is interviewed at Kew Gardens by music journalist John Blake, now a successful book publisher.

'Fool To Cry'

Opposite Ronnie Wood had to learn the riffs and words of over a hundred songs when he joined the Rolling Stones – not only the old hits but new ones such as 'Fool To Cry', which reached No. 4 in the British charts. 'Fool To Cry' was considered sentimental by many fans and Keith is said to have fallen asleep while peforming it at a concert in Germany in 1976.

Above The Nijinski of rock 'n' roll? Mick Jagger seems to have springs on his heels as he gave his all at Earls Court in May 1976. Towards the end of the shows, the band pumped confetti over the audience and threw buckets of water over those fans nearest the stage. Then, naked to the waist, Jagger tipped water over himself too.

Clowns, dragons, cannon fire…

The Earls Court shows, with all the elaborate embellishments of clowns, dragons, cannon fire and wartime-type search lights, established a pattern in which each concert gave fans far more for their money than a simple set of songs, however electrifying the performance was. Every show was to be a spectacle, often themed, as well as rock music at its most powerful, and Mick Jagger was always in control.

Hot in Earls Court

Mick Jagger always gave his all in every show, training like an athlete and, almost teasing, gradually removing items of clothing as the show hotted up. Starting out at Earls Court in a turquoise suit, he was stripped to the waist by the time the show closed.

Opposite top The band is joined on stage by Ollie Brown and Billy Preston at Earls Court on 21 May 1976.

Keith's grief

Opposite top In June 1976 Tara, the ten-week-old son of Keith Richard and Anita Pallenberg, died of a mystery virus. Keith was grief-stricken but insisted that the tragedy should remain a secret for now, and that the current tour should continue.

Above and opposite below Ronnie and Krissie Wood relax at home in Richmond amidst a comfortable clutter of pictures, antique pieces and rugs. Krissie is six months pregnant – a son, Jesse James, was born on 30 October 1976. Ronnie was soon to be involved with model Jo Howard.

Crashing the Bentley

It was a bad start to 1977 for Keith Richard. While he and Anita were still grieving after the sudden death of their third child, Keith appeared in court in Aylesbury, Buckinghamshire, accused of possession of LSD and cocaine discovered by the police in his Bentley after he'd crashed it in the area the previous May. Anita and son Marlon had been in the car with him at the time, and although the car was written off, no one was hurt.

A friend in need

Opposite Here Mick attends Aylesbury Crown Court to lend support to Keith during his current drugs trial. On a sartorial note, Mick's striped purple jacket was worn over green suede trousers tucked into high red boots.

Above Mick sprints back to his gold-coloured Rolls-Royce, attempting to avoid fans and photographers outside the Aylesbury courtroom. No one denies that Keith and Mick have had their differences over the years, but the friendship and loyalties have always prevailed in a crisis. Mick flew in from Los Angeles to help Keith.

Keith in court

Above Keith arrives at the court looking gaunt and understandably apprehensive, and (*opposite above*), dashes away after proceedings end for the day. He pleaded not guilty. His defence counsel suggested that the various drugs found on the night of the Bentley crash had been given to him by misguided fans, and that his client had no idea what the packages contained.

Opposite Mick at the court – it was speculated that he may be called as a witness.

Celebrating a compromise

Above On 12 January 1977 what Keith described as a true British compromise was reached: he was found guilty of possessing cocaine, and fined £750 plus costs, but not guilty of the LSD charge. Broad smiles as he and Mick celebrate at the plush hotel near Aylesbury where they've been staying. However, celebrations were short-lived. When Keith and

Anita flew to Toronto in February to join the rest of the band, they were in trouble again.

Opposite top and bottom On 14 February 1977 Bill and Astrid attend the London wedding of Judy Garland's daughter Lorna Luft and musician Jake Rogers.

Mick joins the Establishment?

While Keith continued to live the life of the rebellious rockstar, Mick joined the cream of London society at the Bond Street Jubilee Ball in Berkeley Square, London marking the Queen's Silver Jubilee, on 7 July 1977. Bianca is not with him, although they are still together, despite persistent rumours about Bianca's friendships with Warren Beatty and David Bowie.

Keith faces serious charges

Ronnie Wood holds aloft an enlarged photograph of Keith Richard who was unable to attend the launch of the band's album, *Love You Live*, at London's Marquee club in the summer of 1977. Keith was in the USA, undergoing rehabilitation therapy for drug dependency, as Mick (*opposite*), explains. A few months earlier Keith and Anita were arrested at Toronto airport and charged with possession of drugs found in one of Anita's 28 pieces of luggage. Some days later quantities of

drugs were found in their hotel room and Keith was charged with trafficking, with a potential penalty of life imprisonment. The whole future of the band was in jeopardy.

At the Marquee Mick denied that he and Bianca were having problems, and said they had no intention of splitting. However, two months later, he heads off to Morocco with Texan model Jerry Hall, until recently the girlfriend of Bryan Ferry, the lead singer in Roxy Music.

Mick's new love

Opposite Mick Jagger and new love Jerry Hall at Heathrow Airport in March 1978 and again (*above*) in October, *en route* for New York. Bianca had filed for divorce on 14 May. Jagger is not the only one with marriage problems – on 19 March Krissie Wood files for divorce from Ronnie, citing Jo Howard in her petition.

Below Bill and Astrid still look to be a solid partnership at the opening of a 'tri-sexual' nightclub in London.

Bianca's divorce proceedings

Mick Jagger, photographed on 3 May 1979, outside the
High Court in London where his preliminary divorce
proceedings are underway. Bianca would have preferred to
have the case heard in America where the financial settlement
might have been more generous towards her.

While Mick is in court dealing with his divorce, Keith is still
involved in legal processes in Toronto. Having been given a
one-year suspended prison sentence, he is now fighting an
appeal against the leniency of the sentence.

Some Girls sells seven million

Opposite top Despite looking relaxed, Mick Jagger was unable to comment about how things were going in the complicated matter of his divorce and the custody of seven-year-old daughter Jade.

Above With a newly grown beard, Mick looks cheerful as he takes a lunchtime stroll outside the court. On 3 July 1979 it was still uncertain whether the divorce details would be resolved in Britain or the USA.

Opposite bottom Bill Wyman in May 1979. The Stones had just given their only live performance of the year in Toronto, arranged by Keith Richards to meet his recent sentencing stipulation. But they did release *Some Girls,* recorded in 1978 despite all the legal difficulties. It was both a commercial and critical success, selling seven million copies in 1979.

Rocket 88 go live

The publicity-shy Charlie Watts sitting comfortably, doing what he likes and knows best. In the gaps between recording and touring with the Stones, Charlie pursued other musical interests. Rocket 88, the band led by Charlie and Ian Stewart, released a live record of a concert in Germany.

Above Keith on stage with Mick in November 1979. Keen to prove there was more to him than bad publicity, he allowed Barbara Charone to write his biography – the first Stone to do so. The ties between Keith and Anita were weakening. Further strain was put on their relationship when Anita was arrested after a teenage boy shot himself in her bed.

1980–84

Bill and Astrid to split?

Above Bill and Astrid on 2 May 1980. Astrid announced with some sorrow that she was considering a split. The couple had weathered many years and she had miscarried several times.

Opposite Mick Jagger on stage at Shea Stadium, New York during a tour of North America.

'Je Suis Un Rock Star'

Opposite Bill Wyman could always rely on attractive female companionship.

Wyman was busy during the summer of 1981 before the band began the North American tour. There were rumours that he was set to leave the Stones. These were in part fuelled by an interview in which he said he planned to quit in 1982 to coincide with the band's twentieth anniversary. In June his solo single 'Je Suis Un Rock Star' was a hit in the UK charts, and he composed music for the film *Green Ice*.

Above Bill Wyman and Astrid Lundstrom were still together on 6 July 1981, despite the reported fragility of their relationship.

Tattoo You was released in August 1981 and was greeted more enthusiastically than the previous album, *Emotional Rescue*. In fact, *Tattoo You* was more a compilation of tracks originally recorded for *Goats Head Soup*, *Black And Blue*, *Some Girls* and *Emotional Rescue*. Mick Taylor, who left the band in 1974 plays guitar on two of the tracks taken from the *Goats Head Soup* sessions.

'Start Me Up'

Above The Rolling Stones opened a North American tour on 25 September 1981 at the JFK Stadium in Philadelphia. Some estimated the crowd to be 90,000 on this blazing day. The band had just released a new single, 'Start Me Up', taken from the *Tattoo You* album. The single sold a million copies in the first week. 'Start Me Up' had been recorded using a reggae beat

during the making of *Black And Blue* and was briefly considered for inclusion on *Some Girls*. The version on *Tattoo You* became a classic Stones' track in the style of 'Brown Sugar' and provoked an instant response from the fans.

Opposite Mick Jagger whips up all his customary crowd-pulling energy. The tour was another mammoth one, finishing three months later in Virginia.

Veterans of Rock 'n' Roll

Mick on stage in Philadelphia – not in bad shape for a thirty-eight year-old. The two-hour stage performances are a physical strain and Mick takes his preparation seriously, limbering up before he goes on stage and running and excercising regularly. Bill Wyman may well be the oldest man in the stadium – he is several years older than the other band members.

'It's A Gas'

It was estimated that the tour grossed $50 million including ticket sales, merchandise and TV and film rights. There was also money raised by sponsorship from the Jovan perfume company, which paid to have its name associated with the concerts.

A film was made of the fifty date tour by Hal Ashby. Mick and Keith assisted with the editing.

Left A long version of 'Jumpin' Jack Flash' is the finale to the show and Mick sings part of it suspended above the crowd.

Birthday Bill

Opposite Mick leans forward, still wearing a yellow quilted blouson jacket early in the show.

Above The man in the white suit is Bill Wyman. The band and their entourage celebrated his forty-fifth birthday in October with a party at Disneyland, Florida.

Ties that bind

Above Bill Wyman and Astrid, seemingly having got through the tough times in their relationship. Bill told reporters that there were still no marriage plans.

Opposite On 9 October 1982 the pair leave London for an eight-week break in Hawaii, which will coincide with their anniversary. It is also a reward for completing a two month tour of Europe, which included the band's first British concert for six years.

Mick in training for European tour

Above and opposite Mick Jagger at L'Escargot, the fashionable Soho restaurant, before a press conference on 28 April 1982. Mick tells an assembly of journalists that the Rolling Stones are planning their first European tour for six years, due to open on 4 June in Rotterdam. He was, he said, already in training for it. Even when pressed he was non-committal about current music trends and about the financial advantages of touring.

Stones get intimate

Above Mick warms up for the new tour with an intimate gig at the 100 Club in London on 31 May.

They had attempted to play surprise concerts at small venues in America in the run-up to the 1981 tour. However, the first show was mobbed by thousands of fans and the performance had to take place outside.

Opposite During the Wembley shows on 25 and 26 June, Mick chose a variety of flamboyant trousers. Keith Richards mostly preferred his trusty beat-up jeans.

'Outstanding' Stones

The band on stage at Wembley. The day before the London dates, Bill Wyman collected a British Music Industry Award on behalf of the band, given for outstanding achievement. Keith Richards was also interviewed on BBC2's *Newsnight* programme.

Stage presence

Ronnie, Keith and Mick form a line-up of almost menacing power at Wembley. The tour closed in Leeds on the night before Mick Jagger's thirty-ninth birthday. About 80,000 fans were at the city's Roundhay Park for the gig. Hundreds of thousands attended the British dates of the tour alone – it was a triumph. Some observers muttered that the long tour had taken its toll and that the band looked tired that night – but the Stones' road still stretched far ahead in 1982.

'Undercover Of The Night'

Opposite top and bottom On stage in Leeds, Mick Jagger's personality certainly stood out. Ronnie Wood was more restrained with a harlequin T shirt to brighten-up *his* image. The night before the Leeds concert the Stones had played to 65,000 people at Slane Castle, thirty miles north of Dublin. The venue was the 1,000 acre front garden of the Earl of Mount Charles.

'Undercover Of The Night' was released in October 1983 and was, unusually for the Stones, a political song dealing with the situation in Latin America. It was not the lyrics but the video, directed by Julian Temple, that attracted most publicity. The BBC refused to show the film, in which Richards plays an assassin wielding a gun. The album *Undercover* reached the top 10 in both the UK and the US.

Above Keith Richards and Patti Hansen. They married on 18 December 1983, Keith's fortieth birthday.

Feeling the strain

Above Just before Christmas 1982 Mick Jagger and Jerry Hall left London for Barbados. Their relationship had ridden a little strain when Jerry had briefly flirted with millionaire race-horse owner Robert Sangster earlier in the year. But Mick is not irreproachable either. When Jerry leaves New York for Paris, Mick (*opposite*) is joined by Venezuelan model, Victoria Vicuna.

Left Bill Wyman leafs through some Beatles memorabilia at Sotheby's, London on 22 December. Wyman was always known to be the archivist of the Rolling Stones.

Top Of The Pops

Above Bill Wyman and Cilla Black at the 1,000th show party for *Top Of The Pops*.

Opposite above Mick and Jerry on their way to a Bowie concert.

Opposite below Mick Jagger and Jerry Hall on their return from Christmas in Mustique, 7 January 1983. Mick is having a house built on the island. In a newspaper interview later that month, Mick talks about the possibility of the Stones breaking up, saying that he doesn't know what goals are left for them.

Charity concert

Opposite above Bill Wyman with new girlfriend Kelly Winn. Stars gathered at the Hard Rock Café for a party after a concert at the Royal Albert Hall in aid of Multiple Sclerosis. Charlie Watts joined Eric Clapton, Steve Winwood, Jeff Beck, ex-Led Zepplin guitarist Jimmy Page and ex-Face Ronnie Lane (who suffers from MS) on stage.

Opposite below Another glimpse of serial travellers Mick and Jerry at Heathrow.

Above A heavily pregnant Jerry Hall and Mick Jagger happily announce that they plan to marry 'any day', although no details are disclosed. The baby is due in February 1984. Ronnie Wood has recently become a father again. He and Jo Wood announced the birth of a son, Tyrone, in New York in August.

Right A relaxed looking Mick on his way to a baby 'shower' thrown for Jerry by the model Marie Helvin, wife of David Bailey.

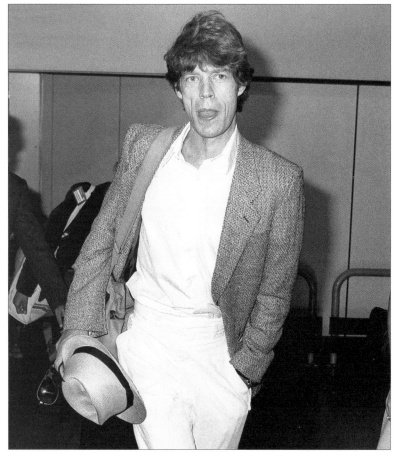

Proud father

Above and left June 1984 and Mick Jagger is enchanted by being a father again. Elizabeth Scarlett, who was about to meet her British grandparents, was born on 2 March in New York, the first of four children Mick and Jerry eventually had.

Opposite above Bill Wyman looks cheerful as he leaves Los Angeles for Miami on 16 January 1984. It is only a few months since he finally split from Astrid, but professionally things are looking up – the Stones signed a $28 million dollar deal with CBS Records.

However, rumours had been circulating for a while about discord within the band. Bill Wyman had been quoted in the *Sun* newspaper as making critical remarks about fellow band members, and had also reportedly refused to help Jagger with his autobiography. News of Jagger's forthcoming solo album caused further speculation.

Opposite below A radiant Jerry Hall after the birth of Elizabeth Scarlett, with Mick Jagger at the Berkeley Square Ball in London in July 1984.

Welcome Elizabeth Scarlett

Previous page and above The christening of Elizabeth Scarlett at the parish church near Mick and Jerry's rented Kensington home on 24 June 1984. Jagger already has two daughters; thirteen year old Karis by singer Marsha Hunt, and twelve year old Jade from his marriage to Bianca. He would later have another girl, Georgia May, with Jerry Hall.

Opposite Baby Elizabeth faces the cameras with her parents. Mick is looking tired.

Mick can't go to the ball

Above Mick Jagger's blue and green suit was deemed unsuitable at the Berkeley Square Ball and he had to go home and change into more conventional attire for the event.

Left Another party and another girlfriend for Bill Wyman, pictured with Wendy Jewel at a nightclub in September 1984.

Opposite October 1984: a sharply-dressed Charlie Watts. Charlie and Ronnie along with with Chris Rea, Andy Fairweather Low and the Who's Kenney Jones, have just recorded an album produced by Bill Wyman, calling themselves 'Willie and the Poorboys'.

Previous page Jerry Hall, flanked by Mick Jagger and David Bowie, celebrates her twenty-seventh birthday at a party at London's Langan's Brasserie. Jagger and Bowie are to collaborate on the single 'Dancing In The Streets' and the accompanying video, which is to be shown at the Live Aid concert in July 1985.

1985-89

Hearing Aid

Opposite July 1985, and Bill Wyman proves his commitment to Multiple Sclerosis research by organising a fund-raising show with fellow musicians Andy Fairweather Low (*right*), Chris Rea, Kenney Jones and Charlie Watts. Following the Live Aid concerts, they call themselves 'Hearing Aid'.

Some of the Stones had played in the Live Aid concert in Philadelphia but not together, perhaps because of the tensions between them. Mick performed solo, backed by Hall and Oates, and also with Tina Turner, while Keith and Ronnie appeared with Bob Dylan.

Right Just back from India in October 1985, Mick Jagger at his garden gate in Kensington and a few days later (*below*), with his agent. In August Mick had a No. 1 single with David Bowie. 'Dancing In The Street' topped the UK charts immediately after its release.

Playing Ronnie Scott's

Opposite below and overleaf Charlie Watts may not look like
a musician, but he's playing at Ronnie Scott's jazz club in
London on 18 November 1985. Mick and Keith came along on
the first night of Charlie Watts and his Big Band's engagement
– a fulfilment of Charlie's long-held dream of playing with top
jazz musicians in Britain's leading jazz club.

Mick Jagger outside his Kensington home on 31 October 1985
and (*opposite above*), with Jerry Hall and the new baby, James
Leroy Augustine, before the christening at St Mary Abbot's
Church, Kensington, on 8 November.

It had been two years since the last Stones album, *Undercover*,
and an unusually long time without recording, but during
1985 the band were back in the studio together.

Farewell to a friend

Left Mick Jagger heads to New York to resume work on the Stones' new album, *Dirty Work*. But Mick, who was concentrating more on his solo career and promoting his own album *She's The Boss*, was often unable to attend recording sessions.

Mick's absence antagonised Keith who felt that the Stones should come first. *Dirty Work* took nearly a year to make and the relationship between Keith and Mick was severely strained. The likeable Ronnie Wood often took the role of peacemaker between them.

Below Along with all other band members and musicians including Eric Clapton and Jeff Beck, Mick Jagger attended the funeral of Ian Stewart on 20 December 1985. Stewart, who had been a friend, colleague and back-up musician for the band since it began, died from heart failure aged forty-seven. The Rolling Stones sang the 23rd Psalm at the service, and later organised a memorial concert at the 100 Club in London. At the end of *Dirty Work* a short piece of boogie woogie piano was added in his honour.

Dirty Work

Above Ronnie and Jo Wood leave for New York where *Dirty Work* was being recorded with their two year-old son Tyrone in March 1986.

There were many visitors to the New York recording sessions, especially around the time of the Live Aid concert. Bob Dylan came along, and Jimmy Page played a solo on 'One Hit (To The Body)'.

Right In April 1986 Bill gets an autograph from Elton John.

Wyman signs

In November 1986 Bill Wyman signed his name beneath Princess Diana's on a petition displayed at a fashionable Covent Garden bar and restaurant. It urged young people to avoid drugs. Other signatories included Cliff Richard and John Entwistle of The Who.

Opposite above Bill pictured in September with teenager Mandy Smith, whom he'd first met two years previously at the Lyceum Ballroom. Their relationship caused a scandal when made public because of her young age, but they would eventually marry in June 1989.

Opposite below Another admirer detains Bill as he leaves Tramp nightclub.

Bill Wyman was less active musically than the other members of the band during this period. Charlie and Mick pursued their own interests and Keith eventually formed a band and recorded 'Talk is Cheap'. But when Ronnie Wood re-united with Rod Stewart and the Faces at Wembley in 1986, Bill took the place of Ronnie Lane.

Christmas in the sun

Opposite above Mick Jagger flew to Barbados, with sixteen year-old daughter Karis for a Christmas break in the sun on 19 December 1986.

Opposite below Early in 1987 Bill Wyman saw a lot of American model Nike Clark. This particular evening they dined at Langan's Brasserie and went on to Tramp.

Above A serenely beautiful Jerry Hall leans against Mick Jagger in Barbados in January 1987. Her thoughts are likely to be on her forthcoming court appearance. Customs officials found a large quantity of marijuana in her luggage when Jerry flew in to the island.

Playboy Jazz

Opposite above Charlie Watts views the cricket memorabilia at an MCC auction at Christie's in April 1987. Charlie was continuing his jazz career, playing with his orchestra at the Playboy Jazz Festival in Hollywood the following June.

Opposite below Charlie buys a distinguished portrait for a little under £1,000.

Left Being a Rolling Stone doesn't open every door. Bill Wyman was refused entrance to Regine's nightclub in London. His crime? Not wearing a tie.

Below Mick *en route* for New York in April 1987, where he was recording a solo album, *Primitive Cool*. Jeff Beck was again to be involved and this time Dave Stewart of the Eurythmics helped with production.

Twenty years on

Left and opposite
After a Tina Turner
concert in London in
June 1987, Mick and
Jerry joined other
celebs including
Joan Collins for a
party at a swish
Knightsbridge
restaurant, San
Lorenzo.

After more than
20 years Mick is still
on the A-list and his
presence at any event
is sure to bring out
the photographers.

Above Bill chats
to Michael White.

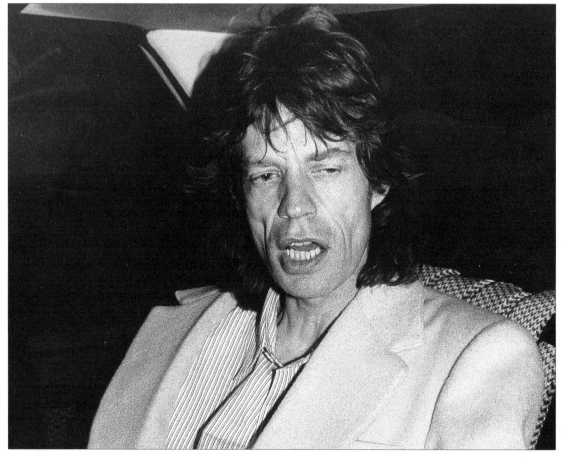

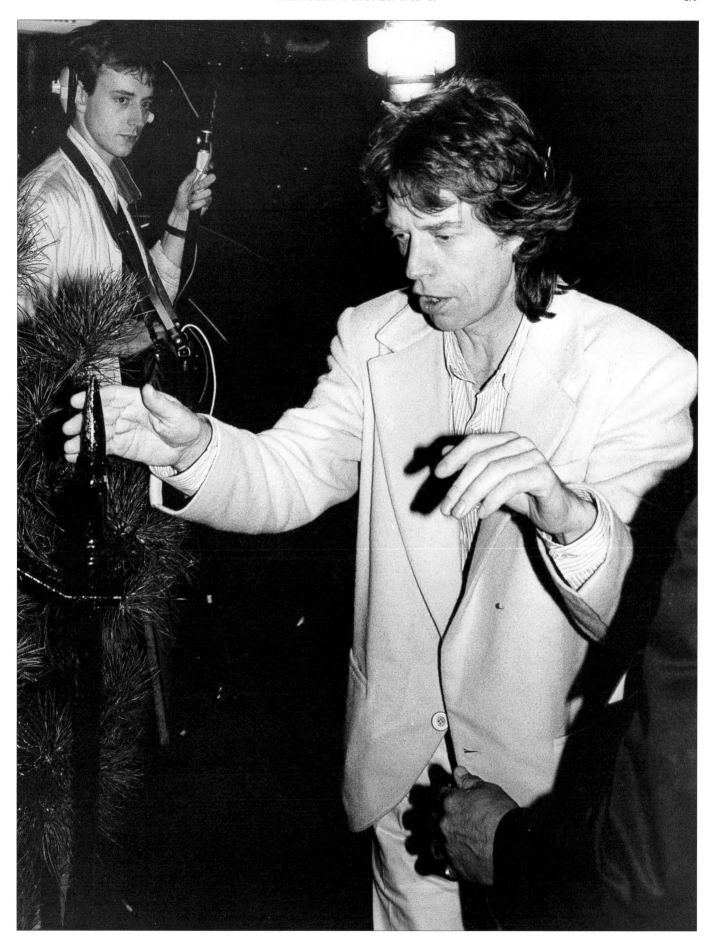

Back live

Opposite In September 1987 Mick recorded his forthcoming single *Let's Work* for the BBC's *Top Of The Pops* – the first 'live' Stones appearance on the programme since 1970. It charted briefly later in the month.

Above and left Bill Wyman with his current date at Stringfellows nightclub in London.

Mandy Smith had announced in August 1986 that her relationship with Wyman was flagging, but it wasn't the end of the road – they announced their engagement in March 1989.

Mick's *Primitive Cool*

Opposite Mick roars. His second solo album, *Primitive Cool*, was released in September 1987. It reached No. 18 in the charts.

Left Ronnie Wood with wife Jo. Even though the Stones haven't been doing much collectively, Ronnie has been busy – there is to be an exhibition of his paintings and he is also involved with his own nightclub and restaurant in Miami.

Below Bill Wyman out on the town with Lorna Luft, who is passing through London.

Ronnie makes an exhibition

Opposite In October 1987 an exhibition of Ronnie Wood's pictures of legendary musicians opened in London. The exhibition, 'Decades', would later open in the USA.

Above April 1988: Instead of performing with the band, Mick has just completed a solo tour of Japan, reportedly receiving £1 million per show. By the time the tour closed, over a quarter of a million tickets had been sold. Ronnie is also on tour in Japan and the two meet up in Osaka.

Working together again

Above Ronnie and Jo Wood in July 1988.

Just when it seemed that the Stones might split, all five members of the band meet for the first time in two years and it is announced in August that the Rolling Stones will record and tour together the following year.

Left Bill Wyman had signed a book deal with Viking/Penguin. He was credited with being the most organised member of the band and having the best memory.

Opposite Mick Jagger on his way to Paris in July 1988. On 26 July Mick celebrated his forty-fifth birthday by dining with Jerry in New Jersey, after her first night in the play *Bus Stop*.

Hall of Fame

Opposite above Ronnie and Jo Wood, *en route* for New York in January 1989, where the band is being inducted into the Rock and Roll Hall of Fame. Bill Wyman and Charlie Watts were absent due to other commitments, but Mick Taylor was re-united with the other band members.

Opposite below Mick Jagger heads for Barbados in February 1989, to discuss a new album and future plans with the rest of the band and their financial, legal and business advisers. In March they signed a multi-million dollar contract – the biggest in rock 'n' roll history – relating to the promotion and merchandising of their next tour.

Mick and Keith settled down to write immediately, and most of the recording was done over a period of five weeks in Monserrat. Bill Wyman had to leave before the album was completed to deal with the press once the news of his forthcoming wedding to Mandy Smith was made public. Although Keith and Mick had patched up their differences, the future of the band was still in doubt because of Charlie's ill health and Wyman's announced intention to leave the band.

Above A photo opportunity at the launch party for boxer Gary Mason, posing with Bill and Ronnie.

Bill's Sticky Fingers

Previous page Mandy Smith, Jo Wood and Barbara Bach, aka Mrs Ringo Starr, party with Ronnie and Bill in May 1989. They were attending the opening of Bill's new Tex/Mex restaurant, Sticky Fingers – named after the band's 1971 album.

Opposite above Bill and Mandy at the launch party.

Above Mandy Smith wears a quiet black outfit for her civil marriage ceremony to Bill Wyman on 2 June 1989. The ceremony was a quiet one in Bury St Edmunds, and was followed three days later by a church blessing in London.

Opposite below Also on 2 June, Mick Jagger arrives late at a party to celebrate the twenty-first birthday of the top model agency Models One.

Princess bride

Opposite Mandy arrives at the blessing at the Church of St John the Evangelist in London. The bride's dress is a £10,000 sequinned lace gown with silk panels of pastel green, pink and lilac.

Above Mr Wyman kisses the cheek of the new Mrs Wyman, surrounded by three perfect bridesmaids and a page – all Mandy's cousins.

Left Keith and Patti Richards were among a huge crowd of celebrity guests at a party at the Grosvenor House Hotel that followed the blessing.

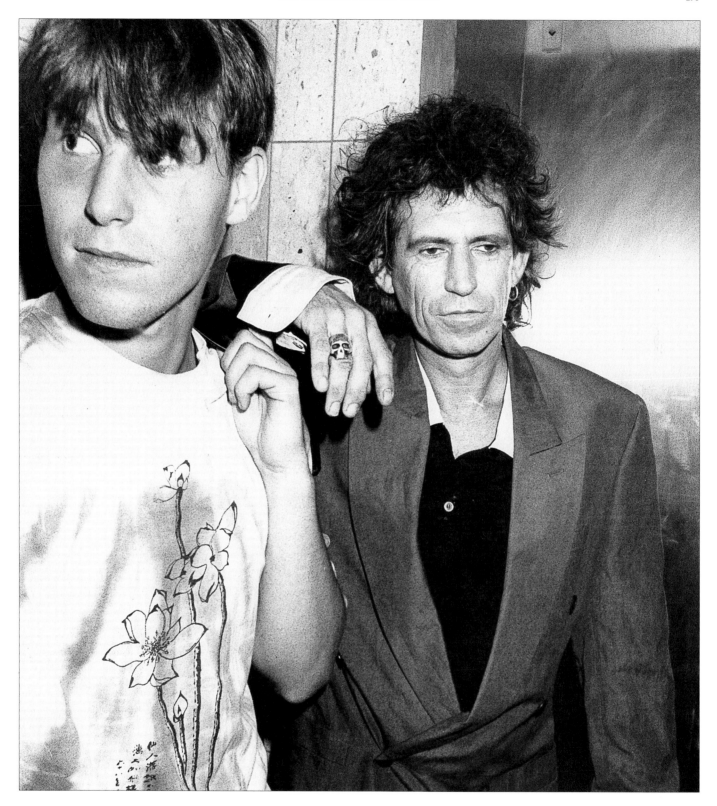

Mr and Mrs Wyman

Opposite above Bill Wyman and new wife Mandy outside Sticky Fingers in June 1989, just days after their marriage.

Opposite below Jerry Hall and Mick Jagger arrive at Bill and Mandy's party. There were more than 500 guests at the celebration, including singers Paul Young and Cyndi Lauper, and comedian Spike Milligan. One of the more unusual wedding presents came from Spike – a walking frame for Bill, 'to help him through the honeymoon'.

Above Keith Richards attends a bash at London's Hard Rock Café with his nineteen year-old son, Marlon in June 1989.

Steel Wheels

The Rolling Stones on the opening night of the *Steel Wheels* world tour in Philadelphia on 31 August 1989. Advance ticket sales for the shows had broken all records. The American leg consisted of 55 dates, finishing in Atlantic City. The album of the same name reached No. 1 in the US charts and No. 2 in the UK. The single 'Mixed Emotions' reached No. 5 in the US charts.

Concert in Philadelphia

Keith Richard and Bill Wyman on stage in Philadelphia. Tickets for the gig had sold for up to forty times the original price on the black market. Ten days later 'Mixed Emotions' entered the British singles charts, reaching a disappointing No. 33.

Show stopper

Above, left and opposite Holding an audience, as ever, in the palm of his hand, Mick Jagger gives a sensational performance in New York in October 1989, fronting the *Steel Wheels* tour, which astonished crowds in every North American city where the band played that autumn. The sets, effects and stage craft almost eclipsed the sheer energy and magnetism of the rock 'n' roll. The New York concert was held at Shea Stadium, home of the Mets baseball team. Seventy thousand fans attended, some over a third of a mile from the stage and depending on binoculars.

1990–2002

Big in Japan

Left and below left On 4 Feburary 1990 Keith and Ronnie leave for the next leg of the *Steel Wheels* tour in Japan. Ronnie is with his wife Jo and children Tyrone and Leah.

Opposite above When Bill and Mandy Wyman celebrated the New Year 1990 at Tramp they took along her mother and Bill's son Stephen. The older woman and younger man were shortly to embark upon a romance of their own. Since their wedding the previous June, Bill and Mandy have only spent five weeks together – both deny rumours of a rift.

Opposite below On 5 March Bill attends his father's funeral at Beckenham Crematorium. Floral tributes were sent by Mick Jagger and Jerry Hall, among others.

Best Single, Best Tour, Best Comeback

Opposite On 8 March 1990 *Rolling Stone* magazine nominated the Stones for a host of awards for 1989, including Best Album *Steel Wheels*, Best Single 'Mixed Emotions', Best Tour and Best Comeback. Later that month Jagger announced a new tour, the *Urban Jungle* European tour. It will feature a new stage set and lighting, and a different playing order from the *Steel Wheels* shows.

Above, left and overleaf The tour opens in Rotterdam on 18 May 1990 and will move to Australia later in the year.

Playing Wembley

Above and left Mick and Ronnie in the groove. When the Stones played at Wembley Stadium on 4 July 1990, there were 'mixed emotions' as some fans had ears cocked to radios, attempting to tune into an England world cup football match. There were several dates at Wembley, and all 120,000 tickets were sold in one day.

Crowd pleasers

During the Wembley concerts the fans' attention was rapturous as the music was accompanied by astonishing visuals including gigantic blow-up dolls during 'Honky Tonk Woman' and an inflatable dog during 'Street Fighting Man'. Mick's many costume changes enhanced the sense of theatre.

Steel Wheels

The Stones were in full throttle during their sequence of gigs at Wembley. The British concerts finished with a date in Glasgow, before the band headed back into Europe, beginning with a show in Dublin.

'Mixed Emotions' is the first track from the *Steel Wheels* album to be released as a single. Mick sings the line 'Lets bury the hatchet, wipe out the past'. Even Keith speculates that it might be about their relationship but Mick maintains this is not so.

Eastern promise

Opposite Mick on stage at Wembley.

Steel Wheels was warmly received by the fans who had waited some time for a new studio album. It was to be the last one on which Bill Wyman played. On the track 'Continental Drift' Mick and Keith returned to Tangier to record rhythms that Brian Jones had introduced them to in the 1960s.

Above The European tour even took in parts of Eastern Europe – here Mick is in Prague, Czech Republic. While in Prague the band were invited to dinner by President Vaclav Havel. Each member of the group was reputed to have earned £10 million from the *Urban Jungle* tour.

Stone Alone at 54

Opposite above Wembley, August 1990 and the band salute the loyal fans. Amongst the crowd of 72,000 were old flames Marianne Faithfull and Anita Pallenberg.

Opposite below Ronnie and Jo Wood in July 1990.

Above Bill at the launch of his autobiography, *Stone Alone*, which covers the period up until 1969, at his restaurant Sticky Fingers, on 24 October 1990. It was also his fifty-fourth birthday.

Mammoth tour ends

Bill Wyman prepares to blow out the candles on his book-shaped birthday cake at Sticky Fingers. The restaurant is decorated with priceless rock 'n' roll memorabilia, including a guitar given to him by Brian Jones and his collection of gold discs.

Right With the mammoth tour over, all of the members of the band take a break. Mick heads for his home in Mustique and Bill Wyman considers his future both professionally and personally.

Having a ball

A 1960s-themed charity ball was staged at the Royal Albert Hall in London on 12 March 1991. Bill Wyman was amongst the 2,000 revellers. His marriage to Mandy was slowly disintegrating and the divorce courts loomed.

Opposite above Bill chats to 60s icons Petula Clark (*left*) and Patti Boyd, the former model who was married to George Harrison and then Eric Clapton.

Opposite below Charlie Watts smiles at the re-launch of his book about Charlie Parker, *Ode to a High Flying Bird* on 3 April at Ronnie Scott's. The book had only sold a handful of copies when first published in the mid-1960s.

Award winners

Left Bill Wyman and Ronnie Wood clutch trophies received at the Ivor Novello Awards ceremony on 2 May. They won the Novello award for outstanding contribution to British music.

Above and opposite below Mick Jagger and Jerry Hall on their way to Nice in 1991, the year after they had finally decided to marry in Bali, Indonesia.

Opposite above Later that month the chestnut trees are in bloom in the gardens of Bill's magnificent house near Bury St Edmunds.

£25 million deal

Above Ronnie Wood's grin is as wide as some of the deliveries at a charity cricket match on 14 June 1991.

Left Mick follows nineteen year-old daughter Karis into a party hosted by former Eurythmics star Dave Stewart.

Opposite Bill Wyman autographs more copies of his best-selling memoir.

The Stones were soon to agree a deal worth £25 million with Virgin records but Wyman did not want to sign. It seemed like he really was getting ready to leave the band.

Base lines

Left Mick Jagger with Dave Stewart at the a party to celebrate the release of Stewart's solo album, *Honest*.

Above Keith Richards takes part in the Guitar Legends festival in Seville, Spain in October 1991. He gets better press coverage than some of the other legends present, including Bob Dylan.

Opposite More book promotion – Bill Wyman with a copy of his book propped on the neck of a double bass.

Baby love

Mick looks thrilled after visiting Jerry and newborn baby son James in hospital in January 1992.

Although there are no plans for the Stones to get back into the studio together, most of the members of the band are working. In 1992 Mick begins his third album, to be called *Wandering Spirit*. Ronnie releases *Slide On This* and Keith will produce his second solo album later in the year.

Bill Wyman seemed to be enjoying some time to rest after twenty years of being a Rolling Stone.

Opposite above March 1992, and Bill Wyman escorts fashion designer Monica Chong at a spring gala wherein British designers raised funds for children's charities.

Opposite below TV presenter Tania Bryer was a guest at Sticky Fingers on 20 May that year.

National Music Day

Opposite Mick Jagger arrives back in the country in June 1992 in order to attend National Music Day on 29 June. He had been instrumental in organising the event, the first of its kind in Britain.

Above Mick Jagger on stage at National Music Day. Thousands of people supported 1,500 events around the country, and singers such as Cliff Richard and Jose Carreras participated as well as rock 'n' rollers like Eric Clapton, Elton John and Jagger. Sadly the event did not become an annual fixture.

Roots

Mick Jagger put the hammer back into Hammersmith when he played there the night before National Music Day in June – it was his first solo concert for two years. The show was a special blues tribute – here he duets with blues hero Jimmie Rogers.

Opposite Mick acknowledges his debt to the other legends who joined him for individual spots, including Buddy Guy and Otis Rush.

Good sports

Opposite Fellow Stones Ronnie Wood and Charlie Watts also took part in Jagger's 'A Celebration Of The Blues'.

Right Bill Wyman, on the outfield at a charity cricket match in Kent on 15 August 1992.

Below The Wood family – Ronnie, wife Jo and children Leah, aged 13, and Tyrone, aged 9.

Ronnie will leave early in January 1993 to give a series of solo concerts in Japan.

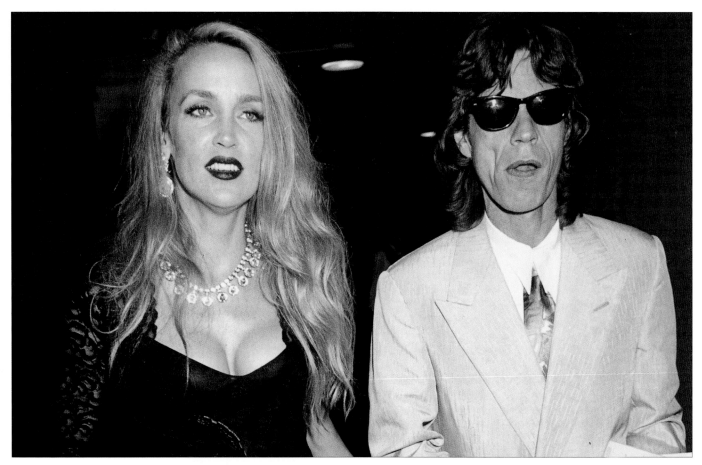

Just Like A Woman

Opposite Bill supports another good cause in attending the premiere of *Just Like A Woman* in aid of the Royal Marsden Hospital's cancer appeal. Princess Diana was among the other guests.

Right However, Bill's concerns were more personal as he was driven to the High Court for divorce proceedings. His marriage to Mandy Smith had been brief and troubled – they had spent little time together due to work commitments and illness.

Above Mick and Jerry had a good night at the Chelsea Arts Ball, also a charity fundraiser, held at the Albert Hall, London in October 1992.

Bill settles

Opposite Bill Wyman looks purposeful yet sad as he strides out of court after the final settlement has been agreed in his divorce from Mandy Smith in November 1992. She had hoped for £5 million but settled for £580,000. Both were sufficiently recovered to find new love before long. Mandy was seeing a professional footballer, and Bill remarried just five months after the divorce. His new wife Suzanne Daccosta, was a Californian fashion designer in her thirties.

Above Keith goes solo – and suited – at a Marquee Club solo gig in London in December 1992. Mick attended but declined fans' entreaties to join his Glimmer twin onstage.

Confounding the rumours

Opposite above Jerry, with Mick at her side, signs autographs at a charity function arranged by Pakistan's cricket captain, Imran Khan.

Opposite left and right February 1993: Mick and Jerry are all smiles, clearly confounding rumours of any estrangement. It was reported that their relationship was in difficulties the previous year.

Above Ronnie at the Brit Awards in February 1993. Paul Young (*right*) was a big star. Ronnie's daughter Leah (*centre*) is set to become one. A few years later she was to appear on stage with the band on the *Bridges to Babylon* tour.

True Brits

Opposite In February 1993 Bill Wyman guested at the Brit Awards. Ronnie Wood was there to congratulate Rod Stewart, his ex-Faces colleague, on receiving a special award for services to the music industry.

Left In March Mick attended a first night party for *Crazy For You*, before joining Keith in the West Indies to start writing for the forthcoming Stones album to be produced by Don Was. Although relationships between members of the band were good, it was five years since they had worked in the studio together.

Below Charlie and Shirley Watts fly into London from New York, in March 1993. Charlie will go on Barbados to meet Mick and Keith.

Fundraising

Left and below Bill is joined on stage by former Amen Corner singer and guitarist Andy Fairweather Low at a March 1993 concert to raise money for the British Lung Foundation. He played classic blues and rock 'n' roll rather than reprise any Rolling Stones songs.

Opposite Mick looking relaxed in April 1993.

While in Barbados he and Keith had written fifteen new songs for the new album *Voodoo Lounge*.

Voodoo Lounge **without Bill**

Opposite The Wood family visit Planet Hollywood, the celebrity restaurant in central London, in May 1993. The members of the band have had time to concentrate more on family life in the last few years but in July they will convene, minus Bill Wyman, in Ireland to begin work on *Voodoo Lounge*.

Above Bill manages to raise a resigned smile after rain stopped play at another of his charity cricket matches, also in May. The downpour at Blenheim Palace was gusty enough to break his brolly as he removed the stumps from the pitch.

Bill leaves the band

Left Bill struck lucky when he married third wife Suzanne. Here they celebrate the fourth anniversary of his Sticky Fingers restaurant. Bill announced in January 1994 that he was leaving The Rolling Stones. His departure from the band was no surprise, as he had dropped enough hints over the years.

Below At a gathering of the clans to mark Mick's fiftieth birthday in July, Mick declined to be snapped but various other band members, including Ronnie in Napoleonic costume, were in the firing line at Walpole House. The theme of the party was the French Revolution – Charlie Watts came dressed as Robespierre, while Jerry Hall was Marie Antoinette.

Having a laugh

Above Ronnie at a party hosted by comedians Peter Cook and Dudley Moore to celebrate the release of a new video. Various Monty Pythons were present, as were golfer Sam Torrance, actor Alan Bates and musicians Dave Stewart and Ian Dury.

Voodoo Lounge

Above Mick Jagger leaving Quaglino's restaurant in London. He had recently returned from a trip to New York to launch publicity for the Stones' forthcoming worldwide tour.

Left Ronnie Wood celebrates his birthday on 1 June 1994 at the 606 Club with Guns and Roses' guitarist Slash.

Opposite above The party continues with wife Jo and Eric Clapton.

Opposite below But by 8 August it was back to work: the opening night of the Stones' *Voodoo Lounge* tour in Washington.

World tour

Opposite Mick and Ronnie on stage in Washington D.C. The *Voodoo Lounge* tour included dates in North and South America, Europe, South Africa and Australasia, with Darryl Jones replacing Bill Wyman. *Stripped*, a live album taken from the tour, sold 3.5 million copies and *Voodoo Lounge* was even more successful, chalking up sales of around 5.5 million.

Above Jerry Hall and Mick Jagger attend a hospital fundraiser in May 1995. The long relationship between Mick and Jerry has endured many ups and downs. Over the years he has been linked with a number of beautiful women but their partnership has remained solid.

Prince's Trust concert

Opposite Ronnie raises a triumphant arm at the Hyde Park concert in June 1996 to raise money for the Prince's Trust. Prince Charles attended and the concert was broadcast to an estimated 120 million people as the Stones and others, including The Who and Bob Dylan, jammed in the open air.

Left Mick and Jerry at a function in February 1997. Just before Christmas Jerry gives birth to their fourth child, Gabriel Luke Beauregard Jagger, in New York.

Below Jerry looks radiantly happy at a theatre awards ceremony in London. Her marriage to Mick was annulled in 1999, but since then they have remained good friends, he moving back into the former 'marital' home for a time after the court case was resolved. Mick attended the West End first night of *The Graduate* in which Jerry took the role of Mrs Robinson.

Artist's studio

Opposite and above Ronnie and Jo Wood live a calmer life these days. In the summer of 2000 Ronnie checked into the Priory to seek help in controlling his drinking. He and Jo opened a private club called Harringtons which sells only organic foods, and Ronnie still enjoys painting, even taking his art materials on tour.

Above Mick presents an award to Kate Winslet. Throughout his career he has displayed an interest in film, although he has not acted for a number of years. He now has a production company, Jagged Films, which was involved in the making of *Enigma,* in which Kate Winslet had a starring role.

Right The Rolling Stones have travelled a long way since 1962, but no one then would have expected that Mick Jagger would be knighted for services to music in the Queen's Golden Jubilee Birthday Honours in 2002.

Long Ago And Far Away

Above 2 June 2002: Charlie poses on his 60th birthday at Ronnie Scott's where he will play later in the day. Although still committed to the Rolling Stones, Charlie continues to develop his private interest in jazz music. In 1996 the Charlie Watts' Quintet issued an album of jazz and swing classics entitled *Long Ago And Far Away*.

Left 27 May 2002: A sombre Mick Jagger draws on the support of his family and the band at the funeral of his mother Eva, who died aged 87. Sixteen year-old Elizabeth stands by her father's side.

Stones go on…

Opposite And so after forty years the band goes on. Each member is allowed to pursue personal interests but they will always be best-known as part of the greatest rock 'n' roll band in the world. Despite their advancing years, they are still capable of drawing record-breaking audiences. The 1997 *Bridges to Babylon* world tour grossed $87 million in the first three months in America, and the Stones are still finding new audiences, playing in Russia for the first time ever in 1998. The new tour which began in September 2002 in Boston was virtually a sell-out three months before it opened. The Stones hold the record for the three most-attended tours of all time: *Steel Wheels*, *Voodoo Lounge* and *Bridges To Babylon*. The new tour will take this remarkable statistic to four.

It seems that the Rolling Stones have no intention of fading away.

Chronology

1936

24 October   Bill Wyman (William Perks) is born in Lewisham, south London.

1941

2 June   Charlie Watts (Charles Robert Watts) is born in Islington, north London.

1942

28 February   Brian Jones (Lewis Brian Hopkin Jones) is born in Cheltenham, Gloucestershire.

1943

26 July   Mick Jagger (Michael Philip Jagger) is born in Dartford, Kent.

18 December   Keith Richards is born in Dartford, Kent.

1947

1 June   Ronnie Wood (Ronald Wood) is born in Hillingdon, Middlesex.

1948

17 January   Mick Taylor (Michael Taylor) is born in Welwyn Garden City, Hertfordshire.

1962

March   Alexis Korner's Blues Incorporated begin regular Saturday night gigs at the Ealing Jazz Club in west London. Mick Jagger and Keith Richards become friends after a chance meeting on a south London train.

April   Mick and Keith meet Brian at the Ealing Club – the idea of forming a band is born. Mick starts singing with Blues Incorporated, sometimes at the Marquee Club in Soho.

May   The band is formed but is not named the Rollin' Stones until June.

12 July   First gig as the Stones at the Marquee. Many more on the London club circuit follow.

December   Bill Wyman considers joining the band, by now called the Rolling Stones.

1963

January   Charlie Watts' recruitment persuades Bill Wyman to enlist with the group. First demo recordings are cut but no record label offers a contract.

April   The Beatles see the band in a Richmond, Surrey club and a friendship is forged while socialising in the Chelsea flat shared by Mick and Keith. Andrew Loog Oldham decides to manage the band.

10 May   Oldham produces the first cut of 'Come On' – destined to become the Stones' first single.

18 May   Journalist Norman Jopling files the first national rave review of the band.

7 June   'Come on/I Wanna Be Loved' is released on Decca, reaching No. 20 in the British charts in August. For their first UK TV appearance the Rolling Stones all wear the same neat clothes. The band continues to perform at small clubs, private parties and halls. More TV appearances follow throughout the summer.

29 September   The Rolling Stones' first tour begins at the Victoria Theatre in London, the band supporting Bo Diddley and the Everly Brothers.

1 November   A second single, 'I Wanna Be Your Man', a Lennon/McCartney composition, is released. It enters the charts on 8 November and remains there for thirteen weeks, reaching No. 9.

28 November   The Stones meet American singer Gene Pitney. Three weeks later his record 'That Girl Belongs to Yesterday', written by Jagger and Richards and produced by Loog Oldham, begins its UK chart ascent.

20 December   The Rolling Stones are voted sixth best British small group in a *New Musical Express* poll.

1964

6 January   The Rolling Stones' second British tour opens in Harrow, north-west London.

17 January   An EP (extended play) is released, featuring five tracks. It spent eleven weeks in the singles charts, reaching No. 15.

8 February   Another UK tour begins, in London. It will close on March 7, just as the band's new single 'Not Fade Away', is released in the UK and the US.

16 April   Decca release their first album, *The Rolling Stones*. On 24 April it reaches No. 1 in the British album charts.

1 May   A third UK tour begins, the day before 'Not Fade Away' enters the US charts. The single remains there for 13 weeks but does not achieve a high placing.

12 May   The band are refused lunch in a Bristol hotel because they are not wearing ties.

19 May   Riots in Hamilton, Scotland, as police attempt to calm 4,000 fans – some with forged tickets – who storm a gig at a local hotel.

27 May   A Coventry headmaster suspends eleven boys who wear their hair like Jagger's.

1 June   The band fly to New York for their first American tour. More than 5,000 fans greet them at Kennedy airport.

5 June   First US concert in San Bernardino, California. A few days later they fail to fill a stadium in San Antonio, where locals profess to prefer their high school band. However, in other cities over the next few weeks the Stones are greeted rapturously.

23 June   British fans riot at London airport as the band returns.

24 June   Rolling Stones voted best British vocal band in a *Record Mirror* poll.

26 June   'It's All Over Now' is released and enters the British singles charts a week later at No. 7, making No. 1 soon afterwards.

8 July   Mick, Keith and Bill attend a party at London's Dorchester Hotel following the premier of the Beatles' film *A Hard Day's Night*.

24 July   A new British tour opens in Blackpool. Thirty of the 7,000 fans present, and two policemen, are injured in the crush.

31 July   A concert in Belfast is abandoned after twelve minutes as hysterical girls are lifted away in straight-jackets.

6 August   The Rolling Stones record an appearance for a networked American TV show. The next day they return to their roots and perform at the Richmond Jazz and Blues Festival, and then record for ITV's seminal *Ready, Steady, Go* television programme.

14 August   The EP 'Five by Five' is released by Decca, recorded in Chicago in June. It is in Britain's singles' chart within days.

Marianne Faithfull's single 'As Tears Go By' is released.

5 September   A new British tour begins at the Finsbury Park Astoria in London.

10 September   The Rolling Stones are voted best British band in a *Melody Maker* poll. 'Not Fade Away' is voted best single.

13 September	Thousands of fans are restrained by rugby players hired as a 'human shield' at a concert in Liverpool.
16 September	Andrew Loog Oldham, 20, marries an eighteen year-old painter, Sheila Klein in Glasgow. The next day police dogs are required to control fans at a concert in Carlisle. In Edinburgh some days later, armoured cars are on standby to protect band members from excited fans.
9 October	The album *12 x 5* is released in the USA, two days before the tour finishes in south London.
14 October	Charlie Watts marries Shirley Ann Shephard in Bradford, Yorkshire.
17 October	'Time Is On My Side' enters the US charts at No. 80. It will remain there for thirteen weeks without becoming a major hit.
18 October	The band is banned from appearing on Belgian TV after 5,000 fans greeted them at the airport in Brussels. Two days later, French fans riot in Paris.
23 October	The Rolling Stones fly to New York for their second US tour.
24 October	Ed Sullivan promises his massive TV show audience that the Stones will never appear again. He professes to be shocked by them.
31 October	After a further series of triumphant and controversial US dates and filming of their slot for the classic film *Gather No Moss*, the Stones greet loyal fans in San Bernardino and go on to many other gigs before the tour ends in November.
20 November	Back in Britain the new single 'Little Red Rooster' goes straight to the top spot in the British charts. The band is simultaneously banned from a BBC radio programme for failing to honour an earlier booking.
12 December	Brian denies rumours that he is leaving the group. The Stones have just been voted best R&B group in a British poll.
21 December	Charlie Watts' book about Charlie Parker, *Ode to a High Flying Bird*, is published.

1965

15 January	*Rolling Stones No. 2*, their second album, is released.
21 January	The group arrive in Sydney, Australia. 3,000 fans welcome them.
22 January	The new album enters British charts at No. 1.
31 January	The Rolling Stones fly to New Zealand after nine sell-out gigs in Melbourne.
15 February	The group flies to Singapore.
17 February	After the final tour date, in Hong Kong, the group flies to the USA.
26 February	'The Last Time' single is released. It will enter the charts at No. 8 and then hold the No. 1 position for four weeks.
5 March	A two-week British tour begins.
18 March	After the tour ends in Romford, Essex, there are complaints when Mick Jagger, Brian Jones and Bill Wyman urinate against a garage forecourt wall.
24 March	The Rolling Stones begin a short Scandinavian tour in Denmark, and go on to West Germany and Paris.
22 April	Start of the the Rolling Stones' third tour of North America.
26 April	The group is forced to leave the stage in London, Ontario, after police turn off the power.
2 May	The Rolling Stones appear again on the Ed Sullivan TV show in New York.
27 May	'Satisfaction' is released in the USA.
30 May	Final date of the tour, in New York. Shortly afterwards, the Rolling Stones beat the Beatles into second place in an American pop poll.

11 June The EP (extended play) 'Got Live If You Want It' is released amidst rumours of Mick Jagger's plans to marry Chrissie Shrimpton.

15 June Beginning of a short tour of Scotland.

23 June Start of a Scandinavian tour, opening in Norway.

1 July It is reported that summonses have been issued against Wyman, Jones and Jagger for their alleged 'insulting behaviour' in Essex on the night of 18 March. On 22 July each would be fined £5.

10 July In a Radio Luxembourg poll the Rolling Stones are voted more popular than the Beatles. Their third album, *Out Of Our Heads*, is about to be released.

1 August Launch of Andrew Loog Oldham's Immediate record label.

20 August 'Satisfaction' is released in the UK, entering the charts at No. 3 a week later. It will spend three weeks at No. 1.

2 September Brian Jones, who has recently bought a house in Los Angeles, counters rumours that the group is planning to decamp to the USA, where they have been recording.

3 September The first of several shows in Dublin, Belfast and the Isle of Man, followed by a new tour of West Germany and Austria.

15 September Fans demolish fifty rows of seats at a hall in West Berlin and then vandalise a train. Four hundred riot police do battle with them. Thirty-two fans and six policemen need hospital treatment.

24 September Start of a 22-date British tour which coincides with the release of *Out Of Our Heads*.

1 October Bill Wyman denies rumours that he is quitting the group.

3 October Keith Richard and Mick Jagger are both injured by over-enthusiastic fans at a concert in Manchester.

22 October The single 'Get Off of My Cloud' is released.

29 October The Rolling Stones open their fourth North American tour in Montreal.

5 November 'Get Off Of My Cloud' is simultaneously No. 1 in the UK and the USA.

14 November An American magazine, *Blast*, suggests that Mick Jagger is leaving the band, just as a new LP, *December's Children*, is released in the USA.

5 December The tour finishes in San Diego, California. Anita Pallenberg flies from London to join Brian who had denied their impending marriage the previous day.

10 December 'Satisfaction' is voted single of the year in a British music press poll and the band is named best R&B group and second best vocal group in the world.

1966

1 January   *Ready, Steady, Go* TV slot.

4 February   Release of single '19th Nervous Breakdown'.

12 February   The group flies to New York for TV appearances, going on to tour Australia and New Zealand.

1 March   Final tour date in Auckland. Later this month Cliff Richard will release the single 'Blue Turns to Grey', written by Jagger and Richard.

12 March   The last of 21 new tracks are recorded at the RCA Studios in Hollywood. Many will be included on the forthcoming album, *Aftermath*.

25 March   Beginning of a two-week European tour.

30 March   Fans in Marseilles take on the police as hysteria mounts during a concert. The group's first anthology album, *Big Hits (High Tide and Green Grass)* has been released.

15 April   Release of the classic album *Aftermath*. One track 'Goin' Home' runs for nearly twelve minutes – unprecedented in pop music. The album will spend seven weeks at No. 1 in the British charts. The single 'Paint It Black' is released in the USA this month.

13 May   'Paint It Black' is released in the UK. It will chart for six weeks, reaching No. 1. Keith Richard has bought Redlands, a moated house, in Sussex.

15 June   Despite a nervous collapse the previous day, Mick Jagger appears on a BBC chat show.

17 June   Chris Farlowe's single 'Out Of Time', written by Jagger and Richards, is released on Immediate Records.

23 June   The Stones arrive in New York for their sell-out fifth North American tour, staying on a chartered yacht in the harbour as so many hotels have declined to take their booking. A British newspaper had reported that the Stones would sue as these restrictions injure their reputations.

28 July   The tour closes in Hawaii, after which the band record in Hollywood and make TV appearances before taking holidays and returning to Britain.

25 August   Mick Jagger and Chrissie Shrimpton escape unhurt from a road accident near his Marylebone flat. His Aston Martin, however, received £700 worth of damage.

27 August   Having hurt his hand on holiday in north Africa, it is rumoured that Brian Jones will be unable to play for at least two months.

23 September 'Have You Seen Your Mother Baby, Standing In The Shadow' is released as the Rolling Stones' new single. Its picture sleeve (a novelty) depicts band members in drag and the record is banned by the BBC. Nonethless it enters the charts a week later, peaking at No. 5.

24 September Start of a new UK tour.

4 November   The album *Got Live If You Want It* is released in the USA, reaching No. 6 in a chart stay of 48 weeks. This month Brian Jones posed in Nazi regalia with Anita Pallenberg. Rumours of their forthcoming marriage persist as the band cuts material for a new album in a Paris studio.

10 December   The band are voted second-best in the world in two British polls. Later that month Mick Jagger and Chrissie Shrimpton part. He is involved with Marianne Faithfull by then. Shrimpton attempted suicide.

1967

13 January 'Let's Spend The Night Together' is released. The single's B-side is the elegiac 'Ruby Tuesday'. Several US radio stations ban the record and Jagger has to sing 'Let's Spend Some Time Together' on an American TV show.

20 January Release of a new album, *Between The Buttons* – all tracks written by Jagger and Richard.

22 January The group appear on the family-orientated British TV variety show, *Sunday Night At The London Palladium*, but refuse to join other stars waving on the stage roundabout which traditionally closes the show.

4 February In Cannes, where Jagger attends the annual music business award ceremonies with Marianne Faithfull, the Rolling Stones are nominated best British act.

15 February Fifteen police officers raid Keith Richard's Sussex home armed with a warrant issued under the Dangerous Drugs Act.

Soon Jagger, Jones, Richard and various women friends head for Morocco, hoping to relax after the Sussex 'bust'. On the way, asthmatic Brian Jones is admitted to a French hospital with respiratory problems.

10 March Brian flies from Nice to hospital in London. By the time he is well enough to join the party in Marrakesh, Anita Pallenberg and Keith Richard have become lovers. Whilst Brian was out recording ethnic music the others flew home from Tangier via Madrid. They left no note.

18 March Brian returns to London. Jagger and Richard are issued with court summonses.

25 March A three-week European tour opens in Sweden and will include concerts in West Germany, Austria, Italy, France, Switzerland, Holland and Poland. There are tensions between the band and police and customs officials throughout as the Stones have increasingly become associated with crowd violence and alleged drug-related offences.

10 May After the first of a series of court appearances relating to the raid at his Sussex home, Keith Richard, and Mick Jagger, are remanded on bail. On the same day Brian Jones is arrested at home in Kensington for separate drug-related offences. He too is given bail.

15 June Jagger and Richard supply backing vocals for the Beatles' single 'All You Need Is Love'. A new compilation album, *Flowers*, is released this month.

27/28 June Jagger and Richards' cases are heard at a court in Chichester, West Sussex. They are both given prison sentences and told to pay costs.

30 June Jagger and Richard are awarded bail and the right of appeal.

1 July A leader in *The Times* reflects surprising public outrage at the severity of their sentences.

7 July Without Brian, who is in the hospital with nervous strain, the other Rolling Stones record. Jones is well enough to join them on 12 July.

31 July In the court of appeal Mick is given a conditional discharge and Keith Richards' sentence is quashed.

18 August The single 'We Love You' is released.

26 August   Mick Jagger and Marianne Faithfull join the Beatles at the Maharishi Marhesh Yogi's seminar in Wales.

14 September When the band members arrive in New York from London and Paris they are questioned by immigration officials about their drugs trials in England.

29 September The Rolling Stones part company with Andrew Loog Oldham.

15 October   Bill Wyman applies for membership of the Royal Horticultural Society.

30 October   Brian is sentenced to nine months' imprisonment for drug offences. He is released on bail from Wormwood Scrubs the next day and on 12 December his sentence is commuted to three years' probation.

27 November   The album *Their Satanic Majesties Request* is released in the USA. It will be weeks before it is available in Britain.

12 December   On the day of Brian Jones' reprieve the Rolling Stones are voted best British R&B group and second best vocal group in an *NME* poll.

14 December   *Their Satanic Majesties Request* enters the British album charts and remains there for nine weeks, reaching No. 3. Brian Jones collapses and is rushed to a London hospital suffering from strain and exhaustion.

1968

13 March   The band are in the Olympic Studios in London, cutting a new album, work which will continue until 18 April.

18 March   Shirley Watts gives birth to daughter Serafina.

11 May   It is announced that Mick Jagger is to star in a film called *The Performance*.

21 May   Brian Jones is arrested for possession of cannabis at home in Chelsea. He denies the charge.

25 May   The classic single 'Jumpin' Jack Flash' is released. It will reach No. 1 in both the UK and the USA.

26 July   The single 'Street Fighting Man', taken from the Stones' forthcoming album, is released in the USA.

17 August   There is speculation that Eric Clapton will join the Rolling Stones now that the 'supergroup' Cream have disbanded.

24 August   Disputes about the 'lavatorial' sleeve of the new album delay *Beggars' Banquet*'s release.

3 September   'Street Fighting Man' is banned in Chicago after political demonstrations.

12 September As Mick Jagger begins work on his film, now called *Performance*, Marianne Faithfull's film *Girl on a Motorcycle*, co-starring Alain Delon, is premiered in London.

26 September In a London court Brian Jones is fined for possession of cannabis.

4 October Marianne Faithful happily announces her pregnancy. Six weeks later and nearly six months pregnant she is taken to a maternity home and loses her baby the next day. Mick Jagger reports that they are both very upset.

21 November Brian Jones buys Cotchford Farm in Sussex, formerly the home of A.A. Milne, creator of Winnie the Pooh.

27 November Fears that the Rolling Stones are to split gather even as the new album is released in North America.

5 December *Beggars' Banquet* is at last released in Britain, with an ironic sleeve spoofing an invitation to a formal party. It enters the charts days later, at No. 3 and remains there for twelve weeks without going higher.

7 December The Rolling Stones are voted best British R&B band in the *NME*'s annual poll.

18 December On Keith Richard's twenty-fifth birthday he and Anita, Mick Jagger and Marianne fly to Brazil to discuss black and white magic with a mystic.

1969

4 January Brian Jones is reported to be 'furious' when hotels in Sri Lanka bar him in the mistaken belief that he is a drifter.

March The band return to Olympic Studios in London to cut a new album. Jagger and Richard work together on new songs, spending time writing in Italy in April.

24 May It is announced that Mick Jagger and Marianne Faithfull will star in an Australian film, *Ned Kelly*.

28 May After a police raid at Jagger's Chelsea home, he and Marianne are arrested for possession of cannabis. They are remanded and released on bail.

7 June Keith Richard's car is written-off after a crash near his home in Sussex. A heavily pregnant Anita Pallenberg sustains a broken collar bone but the baby is safe.

8 June Band members collect at Cotchford Farm and an amicable split is agreed with Brian Jones. Musical differences are cited.

10 June Mick Taylor is appointed as Jones' replacement.

1 July Drug charges against Mick Jagger and Marianne Faithful are adjourned until 29 September.

2/3 July The body of Brian Jones is lifted from the bottom of his swimming pool at Cotchford Farm. A coroner later reports that he had drowned under the influence of alcohol and drugs.

5 July A free Rolling Stones concert in London's Hyde Park goes ahead as planned. Thousands of white butterflies are released as Mick Jagger reads from Shelley in Brian's honour.

8 July Marianne Faithfull overdoses and falls into a long coma in Australia. Another actor takes over her part in *Ned Kelly*. 'Honky Tonk Women' enters the US and UK charts. Two weeks later it will be No. 1 in Britain.

9 July The divorce of Bill and Diane Wyman is announced.

10 July Brian Jones is buried in Cheltenham.

13 July Mick Jagger starts work on *Ned Kelly*. Filming ends in September.

10 August Anita Pallenberg gives birth to a son, Marlon.

12 September Another compilation album, *Through The Past Darkly (Big Hits Volume 2)* is released. It reaches No. 1 and will stay in the British charts for sixteen weeks.

17 October	The Rolling Stones fly to Los Angeles to prepare for their first American tour in three years and to mix the next album, *Let It Bleed*. It will be released in Britain in December.
7 November	This sixth American tour is a sell-out and opens in Colorado.
13 November	Warner Bros waver about the US release of *Performance* because they find the English actors' accents 'unintelligible'.
28 November	*Let It Bleed* goes on sale in the USA and the Rolling Stones are triumphant at a filmed Madison Square Gardens concert. Jimi Hendrix is backstage.
6 December	At Altamont, California, the final concert of the tour descends into tragedy. Three fans die and many more are seriously injured.
8 December	Back home Anita Pallenberg is informed that she must marry or leave England.
11 December	Marianne Faithfull, who was in Italy with her son and a new friend during the recent tour, reunites with Mick Jagger.
19 December	At a London court Mick Jagger is fined for possession of cannabis. Marianne Faithfull is acquitted.
21 December	The band give two Christmas shows at a ballroom off the Strand, London.

1970

14 March	It is announced that the band's first European tour for three years will open in Holland in May and finish in Helsinki in early June. In fact, the tour is postponed for four months.
May	Reports in the British press suggest that Brian Jones' debts were over five times greater than his assets. His estate may be due royalties from songwriting earnings.
24 June	*Ned Kelly* is premiered in London.
28 June	Mick Jagger is said to be dating American actress Patti D'Arbanville.
11 July	Warner Brothers may shelve *Performance*.
31 July	The Rolling Stones' contract with Decca expires. The band are set to launch their own record label.
6 September	Release of the *Get Yer Ya Yas Out!* album which reaches No. 1 and remains in the charts for thirteen weeks.
10 October	The day before the European tour ends in Munich, Mick Jagger visits London with a new girlfriend, the Nicaraguan Bianca Perez Morena de Macia.
20 October	Mick Jagger, cited as co-respondent, is ordered to pay costs in John Dunbar's divorce from Marianne Faithfull.

6 December A documentary film, *Gimme Shelter*, covering the Stones' last American tour and featuring scenes from Altamont, is premiered in New York.

1971

4 January British premier of *Performance*.

6 February A farewell tour is announced amidst expectations that the band will become tax exiles in France. It opens in Newcastle and ends at the Roundhouse in north London.

26 March The Rolling Stones are filmed in performance for TV at the Marquee Club.

1 April The band gives a farewell party in Maidenhead before leaving for France. Band members take up residence in different but neighbouring houses.

15 April 'Brown Sugar' the Stones' next single, is featured on the BBC's *Top of the Pops*. It enters the charts a week later and will reach No. 1.

23 April Release of the *Sticky Fingers* LP.

12 May Mick Jagger marries Bianca in a civil ceremony in St Tropez. Both wear white suits. The bride is already several months pregnant.

28 May Keith Richard has a road accident and will appear in court on subsequent assault charges. *Gimme Shelter* is screened in Cannes.

1 June The Rolling Stones top the British singles and album charts with 'Brown Sugar' and *Sticky Fingers*.

31 July British premier of *Gimme Shelter*.

31 August The four surviving original Stones and Brian Jones' father launch a complex law suit against Andrew Loog Oldham about alleged irregularities relating to earnings derived through their original recording contract with Decca and other rights.

October The mixing of twenty new recorded songs continues and the band plans a new album to coincide with next spring's American tour.

21 October Bianca Jagger gives birth to a daughter, Jade, in Paris.

December The band work on the new album at the Sunset Sound studios in Los Angeles. Mick and Bianca house-hunt in California.

3 December French magistrates accept Keith Richards' defence of self defence after the 'assault' that followed his road accident in May. Charges are dismissed.

15 December Decca release a double compilation album, *Hot Rocks 1964–1971*.

1972

20 February Decca release another anthology album, *Milestones*.

14 April Release of single 'Tumbling Dice' a track from the forthcoming *Exile On Mainstreet* album. It will reach No. 5 in the British charts.

17 April Anita Pallenberg gives birth to a daughter, Dandelion, in Switzerland.

26 May   *Exile On Main Street*, a double album, is released by Rolling Stones Records.

3 June   The seventh North American tour opens in Vancouver. Thirty policemen are injured as 2,000 fans attempt to gatecrash.

31 July   The marathon tour finishes in New York on Mick Jagger's birthday.

9 August   Keith Richard, Anita and their children move to Montreux, Switzerland.

20 November   Mick Jagger sings back-up on Carly Simon's single 'You're So Vain'.

25 November   Band members convene in Kingston, Jamaica for four weeks' recording.

23 December   An earthquake devastates Nicaragua. After Christmas Mick and Bianca Jagger fly there to search for her family and bring medicines. A benefit concert for victims of the earthquake will be announced in the new year. Various fund-raising activities eventually raise £350,000.

1973

4 January   Confirmation of their safety in Managua averts fears that misadventure has befallen Mick and Bianca Jagger.

8 January   Mick's hopes to play in Japan are dashed as an old drugs conviction prevents his entry. A tour has to be cancelled despite record-breaking ticket sales. Even so, three months later the band were voted group of the year and Jagger best vocalist in a Japanese magazine poll.

21/22 January   The Rolling Stones preview their Australasian tour with two concerts in Honolulu.

March   The new album is mixed in Los Angeles.

11 April   The School of Literature at California State University announces that it is to run degree courses in rock music. Amongst the performers whose work is to be studied are Mick Jagger and Keith Richard.

9 June   Mick Jagger denies rumours that Keith is leaving the band. The denial is echoed by Keith two days later.

15 June   Whilst mixing their new album, *Goats Head Soup*, at Island Studios in London, Keith Richard – now domiciled in Jamaica – speaks of plans to record with a rastafarian band.

18 June   Marsha Hunt files an application at a London court, claiming Mick Jagger is her daughter Karis's father. The court orders that blood tests are taken.

26 June   Keith Richard and two others are arrested in Chelsea for possession of cannabis. Keith is also charged with possessing a firearm and ammunition without a license. He is remanded on bail.

26 July   Mick Jagger is thirty. Plans are afoot for a new European tour to begin in September. Bianca will not travel with him. Mick denies their marriage is faltering.

31 July   A fire causes serious damage to Keith and Anita's Sussex home.

6 August   Tickets for the forthcoming UK tour go on sale and are an almost instant sell-out. Further venues and dates are arranged.

20 August   'Angie', recorded in Jamaica is released and will chart at No. 2. Both the single and the album it was cut from will be No. 1 in the USA in October.

31 August   *Goats Head Soup* is released and will hold the No. 1 position for two weeks.

1 September   The European tour opens in Mannheim, West Germany.

7 September First British leg of the tour at Wembley – one of four dates there.

17 September Final British show in Birmingham. The tour continues with concerts in Germany, Holland, Belgium and Scandinavia, closing in Berlin on 19 October.

24 October Keith Richard is fined £205 for possession of various drugs, firearms and ammunition. For her possession of Mandrax, Anita Pallenberg is conditionally discharged.

13 November The Rolling Stones begin new recording sessions in Munich.

1974

5 January Bill Wyman is in Los Angeles recording a solo album. *Monkey Grip* will be released in May on the Rolling Stones' own label.

10 February Mick Jagger once again denies that his marriage is on the rocks.

1 March A film about their US tour, *Ladies and Gentlemen, The Rolling Stones* is previewed in New York.

9 July The Rolling Stones preview 'It's Only Rock 'n' Roll (But I like It)' on BBC TV's Old Grey Whistle Test. The single hit the charts on 30 July, making No. 10.

14 July Not for the first time, Keith Richard jams informally with Ronnie Wood at a north London venue.

27 July Mick answers a Brian Jones fan who expressed sorrow at the Stones apparent indifference to the anniversaries of Brian's death, explaining via a public letter that rather than send flowers to Brian's grave, band members sent donations to a United Nations childrens' charity that Brian had supported.

31 August Keith Richard cheerfully evades questions about his alleged complete blood transfusion in Switzerland.

7 October Mick is reported as saying he only married Bianca because she resembled him. Ten days later, in Paris, he is said to be dating Nathalie Delon.

7 December The band embark on new recording in Munich.

12 December It is announced that Mick Taylor is leaving the band. In the first place he will work with former Cream bassist Jack Bruce. Massive speculation about his replacement centres on the possibility of Ronnie Wood of the Faces joining them.

31 December Ronnie Wood insists that his commitment remains with the Faces.

1975

9 February	After recording in Rotterdam Mick Jagger flies to New York whilst Keith Richard returns to London and works with Ronnie Wood at the latter's home studio in Richmond.
22 March	Recording sessions continue in Munich where the band is soon joined by Ronnie Wood.
14 April	It is announced that Ronnie Wood will join the Stones for part of their new American tour, but merely 'guesting' and on loan from the Faces.
1 May	Central New York is brought to a stand-still as the Rolling Stones perform 'Brown Sugar' from the back of a truck. The tour as planned will be the band's longest ever.
13 May	Ronnie Wood departs to join the Faces for their overlapping tour.
13 June	Mid-tour the band release a compilation album, *Made In The Shade*, on their own label.
5 July	Keith Richard, travelling with Ronnie Wood, is arrested on the highway in Fordyce, Arkansas, charged with possession of an offensive weapon – a tin-opener with a blade attachment. Both are released on bail.

August	The South American shows having been postponed, the tour closes in Buffalo.
13 October	The Rolling Stones and Ronnie Wood begin recording new album material at studios in Montreux. Sessions there finish on 15 November.
3 December	Further recording continues in Munich until 16 December.
18 December	As Rod Stewart quits the Faces, apparently unhappy about Ronnie Wood's frequent 'borrowings' by the Stones, rumours that Ronnie will become an official Stone strengthen.
26 December	American magazines name the Rolling Stones best live band, best R&B band, and best band of the year. Ronnie Wood is most valuable player and *Made In The Shade* is best re-issue album.

1976

26 February	Release of *Stone Alone*, Bill Wyman's solo album.
28 February	It is unofficially announced that Ronnie Wood will join the band.
26 March	Anita gives birth to a second son, Tara, in Switzerland.
10 April	Rehearsals for a new European tour begin in France.
20 April	Release of the album *Black And Blue*. It enters the British charts a week later and reaches No. 2.
28 April	The tour opens in Frankfurt.
8 May	'Fool To Cry' enters the British singles charts. It will reach No. 4.
10 May	The British tour begins with a show in Glasgow.
19 May	After crashing his Bentley in Buckinghamshire Keith, Anita and Marlon are unhurt but the car is a write-off. Police find 'substances' in the wreckage and he is arrested but released as the substances must be identified before any charge is brought. Richard was astonished to learn later that the substances were LSD and cocaine and some newspapers speculated that a Rolling Stone could be used as an unwitting drugs courier.

4 June   Just before going onstage at the Abattoirs for the first of three concerts in Paris, Keith Richard learns that his ten-week-old son Tara has died of a mysterious virus. White and stricken he played on, and insisted that the tragedy should remain secret and that tour plans should not be disrupted.

11 June   The Rolling Stones play in Barcelona – their first Spanish concert. Ten days later they give their first show in Yugoslavia.

23 August   The band performs before 200,000 fans, headlining the Knebworth Festival.

New rumours of tension in the Jagger marriage circulate when they go their separate ways after Mick meets Bianca at Heathrow airport.

20 September   Mick Jagger attends a London Sex Pistols gig at a club. This month he and Ronnie Wood have whittled down 150 hours of live concert tapes for a new live LP.

6 October   Before a magistrate Keith Richard chooses to go to a higher court for his recent charges to be heard. Bail is renewed at £5,000.

30 October   Krissie Wood gives birth to a son, Jesse James.

1977

12 January   At Aylesbury Crown Court, after a three day trial with Mick lending supportive presence, Keith is found guilty of possessing cocaine. He is fined £750 and ordered to pay £250 costs. The following month he is fined a further £25 for driving without tax on the night of the accident the previous May.

February   The first of Keith and Anita's next slew of drug-related travails takes place at Toronto airport, on the way to a short but troubled new tour. Their luggage is searched and Anita is arrested, then released. Days later both are charged with possession of heroin but released, Keith on bail. A court hearing is eventually set for March 14 when Anita is fined $400. For his alleged crimes Keith is remanded on bail.

4 March   Margaret Trudeau, glamorous wife of Canada's premier Pierre Trudeau, throws a party for the band after their opening gig at a small club. As the tour progresses and she parties with them elsewhere, both she and members of the Rolling Stones dismiss rumours of inappropriate behaviour as mischievous gossip. Mrs Trudeau's husband is staunchly supportive of her.

15 May   Touring in Britain Nils Lofgren dedicates his song 'Keith Don't Go (To Toronto)' to Richard whose voluntary treatment for drug addiction renders him unable to attend a Toronto court appearance. It is rescheduled for 19 July when he is once again unable to appear. The case is adjourned to December. Meanwhile German fans raised a collection to help with his fees and plan a demonstration outside their Canadian embassy in support of Keith.

13 September   The live album which will reach No. 3 in the British charts, *Love You Live* is launched at the Marquee Club in London. Keith cannot attend.

23 September   The film of the band in concert, *Ladies And Gentlemen, The Rolling Stones* is premiered at the Rainbow Theatre in London. The band will soon begin to record a new album in Paris, resuming work on 5 December after a break.

19 November   A compilation album, *Get Stoned*, is released and sells well.

26 November Mick Jagger goes to Morocco with Jerry Hall, with whom he will fly to Barbados after Christmas in London together.

2 December Appearing at a Toronto court Keith Richard hears that his trial is postponed. Further delays mean that he will have to wait until October 1978.

11 December As Bianca Jagger leaves London, rumours of a divorce become louder.

1978

27 January Charlie Watts plays with a skiffle group in Swindon.

3 March Recording for the new Stones' album concludes.

19 March Krissie Wood files for divorce, citing model Jo Howard in her petition.

14 May Bianca Jagger files for divorce in London.

19 May 'Miss You' is released. It reaches No. 2 in the British charts.

9 June The *Some Girls* album is released the day before their American tour opens in Florida. 55,000 tickets for the 10 July gig at Anaheim, California sell out within two hours. More than $1,000,000 is taken in advance sales for the 80,000 capacity auditorium in New Orleans where the band play on 13 July.

26 July The tour ends at Oakland, California, on Mick Jagger's thirty-fifth birthday.

20 October As of now, Keith is once again Keith Richards.

22 October Jo Howard gives birth to a daughter, Leah, in Los Angeles.

23 October Keith Richards' trial in Toronto starts at last. He is given a one year suspended prison sentence and ordered to give a charity concert. People incensed by the judge's leniency will begin an appeal for a harsher sentence the following month.

3 December Keith's first solo single, 'Run Rudolph Run' is released in the USA. The UK release in February misses the Christmas rush.

15 December Japan relents after six years and lifts its ban on the Rolling Stones.

28 December The band are voted artists of the year and *Some Girls* album of the year in a *Rolling Stone* magazine poll.

1979

18 January The band convenes in Nassau to cut new album material.

5 April Bianca's lawyers serve divorce papers on Mick in New York.

21 April The Rolling Stones give their only live performance of the year in Toronto, arranged by Keith Richards to meet his recent sentencing stipulation.

4 May Mick Jagger's divorce proceedings begin with a High Court hearing in London. Later that month, in Los Angeles, Mick's lawyers state that the marriage had been over in any true sense since 1973. As an interim measure the LA judge orders Mick to maintain his wife in the 'sumptuous' style she is used to.

18 June The band gathers in Paris to cut a new album. Work will continue intermittently for some months.

27 June Keith Richards' appeal case is heard in Toronto. No decision was made as to whether he should, after all, be jailed.

9 July Bianca Jagger says she would like to continue aid work in Nicaragua but claims she is hampered by difficulty in raising her air fare.

20 July A teenaged boy dies after shooting himself whilst visiting Anita at Keith's New York State home. She would be cleared of any part in his death when the case was heard in November, although she was indicted on charges of illegal possession of firearms.

17 September A Canadian court finally rejects the appeal against Keith Richards' light sentence.

19 October Paris recordings finish. It is planned to release the new album in January.

2 November Bianca is granted a *decree nisi* and custody of daughter Jade.

18 December At his birthday party in New York Keith Richards meets American model Patti Hansen, whom he will eventually marry.

1980

18 February Bill Wyman tells the *Daily Express* that he plans to leave the band in two years' time – their twentieth anniversary.

20 June The single 'Emotional Rescue', taken from the forthcoming album of the same name, is released. It will reach No. 1 and stay there for four weeks. The next single, 'She's So Cold' is released in September but is less successful.

18 September Mick Jagger buys a chateau in the Loire valley.

11 October Recording sessions for a new album begin in Paris.

2 November At a private hearing at the High Court in London, Bianca Jagger's divorce settlement is adjudged. It is thought to be in the region of £1,000,000.

1981

January Mick Jagger flies to Peru with Jerry Hall. He is to star in the Werner Herzog film *Fitzcarraldo* but leaves the project the following month. The entire enterprise had been troubled – not least by Amazonian Indians. Eventually the film is completed and is widely regarded as a masterpiece.

4 March The anthology LP, *Sucking In The Seventies* is produced by Mick and Keith and released on the Rolling Stones' label. It will have mixed fortunes, many American shops refusing to stock it because of the title, and only charts for a few weeks, peaking at No. 17. It will be released in the UK on 13 April.

June Bill Wyman sues the *Daily Star* for claiming he is quitting the Stones. The following month his solo single 'Je Suis Un Rock Star' is released and reaches No. 11 in the British charts.

14 August Rehearsals for a new tour begin in Massachusetts.

17 August 'Start Me Up', produced by Mick and Keith, is released, taken from the forthcoming *Tattoo You* album. It will sell a million copies in the US in the week of its early September release.

25 September The tour opens in Philadelphia before a 90,000 strong crowd.

24 October Bill Wyman's forty-fifth birthday party is held at Disneyland, Florida.

19 December Another tour finishes in Virginia. It is estimated that the band grossed $50 million in ticket sales and earned almost half as much again via merchandising, record sales and sponsorship. A film of the fifty-date tour has been shot by Hal Ashby for release in 1982.

1982

11 January 'Hang Fire' is released in the US.

4 March The Rolling Stones collect a slew of awards in *Rolling Stone* magazine's annual prize-giving. They are voted band of the year and Jagger best vocalist. *Tattoo You* is judged best album and 'Start Me Up' best single. Jagger and Richards are best songwriters and Keith is best instrumentalist. Later this month Jagger and Richards start editing Hal Ashby's tapes of the recent US tour.

26 April The band's first British concert for six years – in Aberdeen. European tour dates in England, Ireland, France, Spain, Holland, Germany, Austria, Belgium, Sweden, Switzerland, Denmark and Italy are arranged.

June Sell-out concerts in London and Bristol. The tour finishes at Leeds.

1 June A live album, *Still Life*, is released.

24 June On behalf of the band Bill Wyman collects the British Music Industry's award for outstanding achievement. Keith Richards is interviewed for BBC 2's *Newsnight*.

1 September Sixty-five firemen extinguish another fire at Redlands, Keith Richards' Sussex home. Later in the month another single from the *Still Life* album, 'Time Is On My Side', is released in the USA. In Britain the song is issued as part of a 12-inch single featuring two other songs. Weidenfeld & Nicolson, the British publisher, signs Mick Jagger for his memoirs. A *Sunday Times* journalist, John Ryles, is engaged to help with the writing in the new year. Towards the end of the month rumours abound that Jerry Hall has embarked on a new romance with millionaire racehorse owner Robert Sangster. They met in June at Royal Ascot.

7 November Recording sessions resume at the Paris studios.

12 November Keith Richards confirms reports in the *Sun* that he and Patti Hansen are to marry. Jerry Hall flies from New York to Paris. The following day Venezuelan model Victoria Vicuna joins Mick in Paris. A double anthology album, *The Best Of The Rolling Stones*, is released this month on a budget label.

1983

14 January Mick Jagger plays the Chinese Emperor in a US TV production of *The Nightingale* by Hans Christian Andersen.

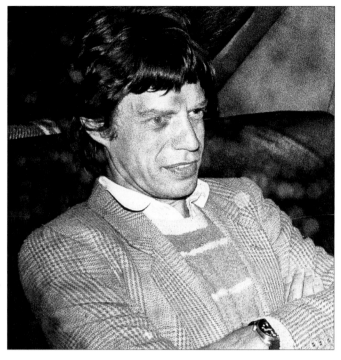

25 January   In a *Sun* interview Mick Jagger talks about the possibility of the Stones breaking up. He tells John Blake that it will disintegrate very slowly and that he doesn't know what goals are left.

25/26 April   To celebrate the 25th anniversary of the Marquee in London, Charlie Watts and Bill Wyman join Alexis Korner on stage.

4 May   Editing and mixing of the Paris sessions begin in New York. Keith joins Mick and Ronnie there.

4 July   Mick Jagger tells the *Daily Star* how he has moderated his earlier drink and drugs lifestyle now that he has to retain peak fitness for touring demands. He will turn forty on 26 July.

20 August   A son, Tyrone, is born to Jo Howard and Ronnie Wood in New York.

25 August   The Rolling Stones sign with CBS in a $28,000,000 deal said to make music business history. Later in August it is announced that Jerry Hall is pregnant and that Bill Wyman is splitting from Astrid Lindstrum, his girlfriend for fourteen years.

20 September   At a Royal Albert Hall concert in London, fundraising for ARMS, the multiple sclerosis charity, Charlie Watts, Eric Clapton, Steve Winwood, Jeff Beck and Jimmy Page join ex-Face and MS sufferer Ronnie Lane on stage. Ten months later a live album, *The Ronnie Lane Appeal to ARMS*, is released.

18 October   Shooting for a video to accompany the next single, 'Undercover Of The Night', begins. It will continue in Mexico City.

30 October   'Undercover Of The Night' is released. A week later the album, *Undercover*, is released on Rolling Stones Records. Three days later the BBC bans the video and the next day Mick Jagger defends it on a Channel 4 youth programme, *The Tube*. The single will reach No. 12 in the British charts and the album *Undercover* No. 1.

9 December   Final date of a short US tour to raise cash for ARMS, in New York.

18 December   On his fortieth birthday Keith Richards marries Patti Hansen in Mexico.

1984

23 January   New single 'She Was Hot' is released. It dips into the UK charts at No. 40 and only makes No. 44 in the US listings, possibly hindered by the banning of a raunchy video which featured the trouser flies of band members popping open.

2 March   A daughter, Elizabeth Scarlett, is born to Jerry Hall and Mick Jagger in New York.

27 March   Critical remarks made by Bill Wyman about band members are published in the *Sun*. A week later he denies having made them.

6 May   Mick Jagger begins working on a song, 'State Of Shock', with Michael Jackson in New York. It is released in June, reaching No. 3 in the US charts and No. 14 in Britain in July.

29 June   *Rewind*, a compilation LP, is released and reaches No. 12 in the UK charts.

23 July   News of Mick Jagger's forthcoming solo album causes speculation about fractures within the band. He offers assurances that the Stones are very much together still and planning a new tour.

August   Decca release the *Beggar's Banquet* LP, re-mastered and with its original sleeve.

September   Tour plans are postponed because of Mick Jagger's solo schedules. Bill Wyman produces an LP by Willie and the Poor Boys, featuring Charlie Watts and other musicians.

October   Mick Jagger declines £1,000,000 to appear on TV in *Dallas*.

November	Band members meet in Amsterdam to discuss their future. Mick, Jerry and film/video producer Julian Temple fly to Rio de Janeiro to shoot a promo video for Jagger's new album.
28 November	An exhibition of Ronnie Wood's portraits of musicians and friends opens in Dallas. The show runs well into the new year.

1985

3 January	Ronnie Wood and Jo Howard marry in Denham, Buckinghamshire. All the other Stones, except Mick Jagger, attend. Later that month Mick and Keith begin work for the new Stones' LP at the Pathe Marconi Studios in Paris.
4 February	Mick Jagger's first solo single, 'Just Another Night', is released in the UK and US. It is taken from his forthcoming album, *She's The Boss* and will reach No. 27 in the UK singles charts.
18 March	Patti Richards gives birth to Theodora Dupree in New York.
11 April	Just after Mick Jagger begins work on the video for his next single, 'Lucky In Love' (to be released on April 19), the band resume work in Paris on their next album. Thirty tracks are recorded by the end of June. Release has been delayed to September.

13 July	The Live Aid concerts take place in London and Philadelphia, broadcast to a global audience of 1.6 billion. The Rolling Stones as such do not take part but Mick, Keith and Ronnie all separately play their parts.
19 August	Charlie Watts breaks his leg in three places after a fall at home in Devon.
23 August	The single of Mick Jagger duetting with David Bowie on 'Dancing In The Street' is released worldwide and becomes a disco classic, thanks partly to an inspired video. It is immediately No. 1 in the UK charts. There are intriguing rumours of Jagger and Bowie reprising the Tony Curtis/Jack Lemmon roles in a remake of *Some Like It Hot*.
28 August	James Leroy Augustine is born to Mick Jagger and Jerry Hall in New York.
18 November	Charlie Watts, who has been developing his early jazz interest, opens for a week at Ronnie Scott's club in London with his 29-piece Big Band. Jack Bruce and Stan Tracey are amongst the musicians. Performances are attended by Keith, Mick and Bill.
25 November	Work on the new album resumes in New York. A few days later Mick Jagger sings 'Honky Tonk Women' with Tina Turner in Carolina.
12 December	Ian Stewart, friend, colleague, some-time back-up musician and management stalwart dies of a heart attack in London, aged 47. His funeral on 20 December is attended by all the Rolling Stones and his death may account for the restrained birthday party held by Keith Richards on 18 December. On 23 February 1986 the band played at an invitation-only memorial gig for Ian Stewart at the 100 Club in London.

1986

25 February	The Rolling Stones are given a Lifetime Achievement Award at the Grammies in Los Angeles, presented to them by Eric Clapton.
3 March	Latest single 'Harlem Shuffle' is released. It will reach No. 7 in the British charts and No. 5 in the USA.
24 March	The new album, *Dirty Work* is released. It enters the British charts in April and will reach No. 3.

11 April   *USA Today* runs a story over the next three days concerning tensions between Mick Jagger and Keith Richards, and saying that Mick has not been available to promote *Dirty Work* because commitments on his solo recording come first.

19 April   The Charlie Watts Orchestra begins a week's engagement at Ronnie Scott's club.

1 May   The band convenes at Elstree Studios, north of London to shoot a video for their next single, 'One Hit To The Body'. The record is released on 19 May.

20 June   Before the Prince and Princess of Wales, Mick Jagger – along with David Bowie, Elton John, Paul McCartney, Phil Collins, Eric Clapton and Tina Turner – takes part in a fundraiser for the Prince's Trust. Earlier in the month Ronnie Wood, and Keith Richards have been busy with separate musical commitments in the USA.

5 July   Ronnie Wood and Bill Wyman join Rod Stewart on stage for a Faces reunion concert at Wembley.

12 July   Keith discusses a possible film project with Chuck Berry in St Louis.

15/16/17 July   Keith Richards joins Bob Dylan for concerts at Madison Square Garden, New York.

31 July   Mick Jagger's single 'Ruthless People', theme song for a Disney film of the same name, is released. It has modest chart success.

26 July   Patti Richards' daughter, Alexandra Nicole, is born in New York.

3 August   Sixteen-year-old Mandy Smith speaks to a British newspaper about her relationship with Bill Wyman. It has lasted for over two years and now she is tiring of it.

29 August   A version of 'Jumpin' Jack Flash', recorded by Aretha Franklin and produced by Ronnie and Keith, is released. It will reach No. 21 in the US charts in September.

15 September   Mick discusses plans for his next album with Dave Stewart of the Eurythmics, in Los Angeles. Recording for the album will begin in Holland in November.

November   Charlie Watts and his 33-piece orchestra arrive in New York for a short East Coast tour.

3 December   Keith Richards flies in from Jamaica to catch the orchestra play at the Ritz.

1987

21 January   Jerry Hall is arrested at the airport in Barbados, charged with importing marijuana. Some hours later she is released on bail.

20 February   After two adjournments Jerry Hall is finally found not guilty. She and Mick fly to New York where work on his solo album continues. Both Keith Richards and Ronnie Wood concurrently work on their albums.

13 April   Bill Wyman launches his AIMS project in London.

13 June   Charlie Watts and his orchestra play at the Playboy Jazz Festival in Hollywood.

13 July   Keith discusses a Virgin solo deal with Richard Branson. It is signed on 17 July.

31 August	Mick Jagger's single 'Let's Work' is released, reaching No. 35 in UK.
14 September	Mick Jagger's album, *Primitive Cool*, is released. It will reach No. 18 in the British charts.
27 September	A British newspaper suggests that some tracks on Mick's album contain critical messages about Keith.
29 October	An exhibition of Ronnie Wood's paintings of legendary musicians opens in London. Two days later he flies to Miami, checking progress on his night club and restaurant.
4 November	Ronnie Wood opens a North American tour in Columbus, Ohio.
14 November	The entire Stones back catalogue is re-released by CBS.
19 December	Ronnie Wood and Bo Diddley play at the opening of Woody's On The Beach in Miami.

1988

7/8 January	Mick Taylor joins Ronnie onstage at the Miami club.
20 January	At the annual Rock 'n' Roll Hall of Fame in New York, Mick Jagger jams with Bruce Springsteen and George Harrison, and also with both Bob Dylan and Jeff Beck. He sings 'Satisfaction' solo.
20 February	Bill Wyman and Ronnie Wood join Phil Collins, Eddy Grant, Ian Dury, Kenney Jones, Elvis Costello and Chris Rea at a Royal Albert Hall benefit that Bill has arranged for the Great Ormond Street children's hospital.
12 March	Mick Jagger and Ronnie Wood meet at the former's hotel in Osaka. Both are in Japan on separate tours. Mick is reputed to receive £1,000,000 for each of his sell-out shows.
25 March	By the time the Jagger tour closes in Nagoya, over a quarter of a million tickets have been sold. Before leaving Japan he guests with Tina Turner at her own concert in Osaka.
26 April	Mick Jagger is cleared of copyright infringement charges regarding a song called 'Just Another Night', on his *She's The Boss* album.
18 May	All five members of the Rolling Stones meet for the first time in two years, at a London hotel. Plans for working together again and touring are discussed.

22 July	Bill Wyman's book deal with Viking/Penguin is announced.
26 July	Mick Jagger celebrates his 45th birthday and Jerry's first night in *Bus Stop* at a theatre in New Jersey. They dine after the show.
22 August	Mick Jagger announces the Stones will record and tour together the following year. 'Satisfaction' is voted best single of the last 25 years by *Rolling Stone* magazine.
24 August	Upon arrival in Australia for his solo tour Mick Jagger says he will stop touring when he hits fifty.
4 October	Virgin release *Talk Is Cheap*, Keith Richards' first solo album.
16 October	Keith Richards, whose own home has been damaged in the recent hurricane, plays at the fundraising Smile Jamaica concert in London.
16 November	Ronnie Wood receives undisclosed libel damages after an erroneous newspaper report suggested he had been unfaithful to his wife.
24 November	Keith Richards and his band the X-Pensive Winos open their US tour in Atlanta.

1989

January	Mick Jagger and Keith Richards plan the new Stones album in Barbados.
18 January	At the New York Hall of Fame awards the band is inducted. Bill and Charlie are absent but Mick Taylor joins the others.

19 January   Charlie Watts joins Mick, Keith and Ronnie in New York to make plans.

18 February   The Stones' financial, legal and business advisers join Jagger and Richards in Barbados. Charlie Watts arrives two days later. Bill is giving a charity concert in Britain but he and Ronnie Wood join the others in early March.

15 March   The band sign a multi-million dollar contract – the biggest in rock and roll history – relating to promotion and merchandising of their next tour, for which over fifty dates are proposed.

28 March   Recording a new album begins in Montserrat.

31 March   Mandy Smith announces her engagement to Bill Wyman.

9 May   Party to launch the opening of Bill Wyman's restaurant, Sticky Fingers, in Kensington. Montserrat recordings completed, this month sees the mixing of the new album in London.

11 May   Bill Wyman captains the team he has assembled for a showbusiness charity cricket match in aid of terminally ill children.

17 May   A newspaper reports an altercation between Charlie Watts and Mick Jagger, in Amsterdam, where the band have gathered for group discussion.

2 June   Bill Wyman marries Mandy Smith quietly in Bury St Edmunds. Three days later the marriage is blessed in London and a reception is held at the Grosvenor House Hotel. Mick Jagger gives the couple a £200,000 Picasso etching.

11 July   The Stones announce the *Steel Wheels* tour at a press conference at Grand Central Station, New York. There will be an album of the same name. Advance ticket sales for the tour break all records. The band and their entourage set up elaborate camp in Washington, Connecticut.

17 August   A new single, 'Mixed Emotions', is released. It reaches No. 5 in the US.

31 August   Tour opens in Philadelphia. Black market tickets sell for up to forty times the original price.

9 September   'Mixed Emotions' enters the British charts, reaching No. 33.

19 December   Final North American date of the tour, in Atlantic City.

1990

February   The Stones tour Japan for the first time.

14 February   First of the *Steel Wheels* dates in Tokyo.

8 March   *Rolling Stone* magazine nominates the Stones as best band and artists of the year for 1989, *Steel Wheels* best album and 'Mixed Emotions' best single. Mick Jagger is nominated best male singer, Bill Wyman best bassist and Charlie Watts best drummer.

22 March   Mick Jagger announces the *Urban Jungle* European tour in London. It will feature a new stage set and lighting and a different playing order from the *Steel Wheels* shows. By the following day 120,000 tickets for the Wembley concerts have sold out.

18 May   The tour opens in Rotterdam and moves on through France, Germany, Portugal, Spain, Ireland, Italy, Austria, Sweden, Norway and Denmark.

July   Release of *Voodoo Lounge* album.

4 July   British concerts (between shows in Paris and Dublin), open with several at Wembley and one in Glasgow.

9 August   The European leg of the tour closes in Copenhagen.

September/ October   The tour continues in Australia.

17 January	Keith Richards' *Main Offender* tour opens in Seattle.
9 February	Mick Jagger's third solo album, *Wandering Spirit*, is released.
16 February	Bill Wyman stands in for ailing bassist Ronnie Lane at a Faces reunion performance at London's Brit Awards, joining Rod Stewart, Ronnie Wood, Kenney Jones and Ian McLagan onstage.
April	Mick Jagger and Keith Richards fly to Barbados to begin writing songs for a new album and are shortly joined by Charlie Watts.
9 July	The band begin recording in Ireland.
12 October	The Charlie Watts Quintet release their collection *Warm & Tender*.
28 November	Virgin release *Jump Back*, an 18-track greatest hits CD compilation.

1991

1 March	Julian Temple directs the *Highwire* video in New York.
2 April	The Stone's fifth live album, *Flashpoint*, is released.
2 May	The Rolling Stones are honoured at the Ivor Novello Awards in London for their outstanding contribution to British music.
19 November	The Rolling Stones sign to Virgin Records.
10 December	Keith Richards and the X-Pensive Winos' live album is released on CD and video.

1992

The Rolling Stones do not tour or release an album this year.

August	Ronnie Wood's solo album, *Slide On This*, is released.
20 October	Keith Richards' second solo album, *Main Offender*, is released by Virgin.
27 November	Keith and the Winos begin a short European tour.
31 December	Keith and his band play at a small New York venue.
	Bill Wyman and Mandy Smith divorce.

1993

10 January	Ronnie Wood gives the first of four solo concerts in Japan.

1994

January	Bill Wyman leaves the Rolling Stones. Only three original band members now remain – but they seem perfectly happy to convene for long tours, even if the days of mega-success in the singles charts are over. Bassist Darryl Jones replaces Bill Wyman for the 1994/5 *Voodoo Lounge* world tour.
	The Rolling Stones pick up an MTV Lifetime Achievement Award and a *Billboard* Award for Artistic Excellence.
	The two-year *Voodoo Lounge* tour opens.
10 November	The Rolling Stones are the first rock and roll band to broadcast live on the internet.

1995

January	The South American leg of the tour opens with concerts in Mexico and Argentina. Shows in South Africa, Japan and Australasia follow.
3 June	Bob Dylan joins the band onstage in Stockholm for a rendition of 'Like A Rolling Stone'.
30 August	Tour closes in Rotterdam. Live recordings made during the tour form the album *Stripped*, released later in the year.

1996

The Rock 'n' Roll Circus album is released. Charlie Watts' quintet release *Long Ago And Far Away*, an album of jazz and swing classics. Keith Richards works on a solo album.

1997

August   The *Bridges To Babylon* tour is announced.

23 September Tour opens in Chicago and goes on to thirty-two other cities in North America. Young Leah Wood, Ronnie's daughter, guests with the band when they take the tour to Wembley.

October   Bill Wyman announces the formation of a new band, The Rhythm Kings. Their first album, *Struttin' Our Stuff*, features guest musicians Eric Clapton, Albert Lee, Georgie Fame and Peter Frampton.

16 October   Bill Wyman's first live performance since leaving the Rolling Stones – at the Forum in north London.

8 December   Jerry Hall gives birth to Gabriel Luke Beauregard Jagger in New York – the couple's fourth child and second son.

18 December   It is announced that so far the *Bridges To Babylon* tour of North America has grossed nearly $87 million – a box office record.

1998

23 April   The tour closes with a last show in Chicago – where it had started months earlier.

11 August   The Rolling Stones play in Moscow for the first time.

2 November   The album *No Security*, recorded live at an Amsterdam concert, is released.

1999

January   Jerry Hall files for divorce from Mick Jagger. In the end she won an annulment as the Bali marriage was not recognised by the courts. Afterwards she said Mick's settlement was 'very generous'.

10 June   The Rolling Stones play slightly longer than agreed at a small venue in west London and are fined £50,000 for breaching regulations.

9 July   In a new book, *Death Of A Rolling Stone*, author Anna Wohlin (Brian Jones' girlfriend at the time of his death) asserts that he was murdered.

27 July   DNA tests confirm that Mick Jagger is the father of Luciana Morad's baby son, Lucas.

October   Mick Jagger resumes residence in his former 'marital' home with Jerry Hall. The couple live amicably in separate parts of the house.

13 November A re-mix of 'It's Only Rock 'n' Roll' is released as a Christmas single, with proceeds going to charity.

26 November A landlord defeats Mick Jagger and Keith Richards in the High Court after the Stones attempt to sue him for exploitation because he named his pub 'Rolling Stone'.

2000

3 January   '(I Can't Get No) Satisfaction' topped a US poll of the 100 greatest rock songs of all time.

16 January   A spokesman for Britain's Prime Minister Tony Blair denies that Downing Street had vetoed a knighthood for Mick Jagger in the Queen's New Year's honours, in which both Elton John and Paul McCartney were knighted.

28 March   Mick Jagger returns to his old school Dartford Grammar to open a new arts centre named after him.

May	Mick, Ronnie, Charlie and Keith play at a private pub gig in south London – a wake for the band's long-term employee Joe Seabrook who died shortly before, aged 58.
27 May	Band members convene at the funeral of Eva Jagger, Mick's 87 year-old mother.
30 June	Ronnie Wood checks into the Priory Clinic in south London, often used by celebrities keen to kick addictions. He was to call 'time' at his private pub in the grounds of his house in Ireland.
3 July	Mick Jagger and Marsha Hunt attend the wedding of their daughter Karis, in San Francisco.
2 December	Jade Jagger and her two children survive a car crash near their home in Ibiza. Both Mick and Bianca Jagger rush to them and charter a jet to take them to Britain for treatment.

This year Andrew Loog Oldham's memoirs, *Stoned*, are published, offering cheerfully unrepentant insights into the Stones' early years. Its author, now a Scientologist and living in Bogota, expresses no regret whatsoever about his parting of the ways with the band he helped to create.

Jerry Hall appears as Mrs Robinson in *The Graduate* in London's West End.

2001

March	Britain's *Sun* newspaper reports a rift between Mick and Keith – the latter apparently worried that Mick is more interested in pursuing film projects than getting back on the road.
August	Bono, Pete Townsend and Missy Elliott, amongst others, join Mick Jagger in the studio as he records his next solo album, *Goddess In The Doorway*.
23 October	Mick Jagger announces that the Stones will tour again – but first he has to promote *Goddess In The Doorway*.

2002

May	A new Rolling Stones tour is announced in New York. It is set to open in Boston in September.
31 May	Plans for *The Rolling Stones Remastered* series are announced. Twenty-two classic albums, various compilations and some singles are to be re-formatted for today's advanced home music technology.
9 June	Michael Phillip Jagger is knighted for services to music in the Queen's Golden Jubilee Birthday Honours.

Bibliography

Days in the Life, Jonathon Green, Pimlico, London, 1998

The Stones, Philip Norman, Sidgwick and Jackson, London, 2001

A Life on the Road, ed Jools Holland and Dora Lowenstein, Virgin, London, 1998

The Rolling Stones, Robert Palmer, Sphere, London, 1984

Up and Down with the Rolling Stones, Tony Sanchez & John Blake, Blake, London, 1991

The Rolling Stones Chronicle, Massimo Bonanno, Plexus, London, 1990

The Rolling Stones Rip This Joint, Steve Appleford, Thunder's Mouth Press, New York, 2000

Complete Guide to the Music of the Rolling Stones, James Hector, Omnibus Press, London, 1995